wrapped

CRÊPES, WRAPS AND ROLLS
YOU CAN MAKE AT HOME

GAITRI PAGRACH-CHANDRA

PHOTOGRAPHY BY KEIKO OIKAWA

PAVILION

First published in 2014
by Pavilion Books
10 Southcombe Street
London W14 0RA

An imprint of
Anova Books Company Ltd

www.anovabooks.com

ISBN: 9781909108776

A CIP catalogue record for this book is
available from the British Library

10 9 8 7 6 5 4 3 2 1

Reproduction by Mission, Hong Kong
Printed by Toppan Leefung Printing Ltd, China

Commissioning editor: Emily Preece-Morrison
Art direction: Anova Books Design Team
Layout designer: Anna Perotti
Photographer: Keiko Oikawa
Home economist: Aya Nishimura
Stylist: Jo Harris
Copy editor: Kathy Steer
Production: Laura Brodie

NOTES

All spoon measurements are level.
1 teaspoon = 5ml; 1 tablespoon = 15ml.

Free-range eggs are recommended.
Note that some recipes contain raw
or lightly cooked eggs. The young,
elderly, pregnant women and anyone
with an immune-deficiency disease
should avoid these, because of the
slight risk of salmonella.

To sterilize jars for pickles, sauces and
jams, put the jars in a preheated oven at
150°C/300°F/Gas Mark 2 for 20 minutes.

CONTENTS

BEFORE YOU START

▲▲▲▲▲▲▲▲▲▲▲▲▲▲▲▲▲▲▲▲▲▲▲▲▲▲▲▲▲▲

If you've never come across my work before, perhaps you might like to know a little about me, as it explains a great deal about my writing. My ancestors sailed from India many generations ago, to work as indentured labourers in the sugar industry in what was then British Guiana, now simply Guyana. Time passed and conditions improved, and none of them felt the need to make use of the repatriation clause in their contracts. I was brought up in happy circumstances on sugar plantations, in a quaintly colonial style. Later I left to study political science and modern languages in Canada and Spain. After university, I married a Dutchman and have lived in Holland ever since. I have always travelled a lot and regularly visit good friends in many parts of the world who share my passion for food and food culture. The recipes in this book reflect all of these things.

This is a book for people who want flavourful food that can be prepared in a reasonable amount of time with readily available ingredients. You will find an eclectic mix of food from all over the world. I like to think of it as vibrant food: street food, snack food and finger food, mostly in a wrapped form, for you to make and eat when the mood takes you. To me, this is food that serves many purposes. It will celebrate fine weather and long balmy evenings outdoors, but will also brighten your home with splashes of colour and flavour on dreary days, or whenever you need a cheering bite. For some, it will bring back pleasant memories of holidays abroad.

Whether you're single or a couple, whatever your age, and even if you are an average-sized or large family, I hope you'll find something here that makes you feel like cooking it. I'm handing you the building blocks with some tips and suggestions to get you started. Wander through the chapters and combine the dishes as you wish, using the wrapper or bread of your choice with fillings and accompaniments to suit. Eat the fritters and savoury cakes as they are, or stuff them into a wrapper if you prefer; some make good vegetarian options. I have given snack-sized portions, but you can easily double or treble recipes if that suits your situation better. For instance, four wraps will make a good snack for the same number of people. Two per person will make a fine meal for two, and you can add salads, relishes and components from other chapters to keep on extending it, until you have quite a heavily laden table – a feast, in fact. It's all up to you. The recipes are almost all quick (if you discount marinating times) and easy, or as easy as I can make them while preserving the original flavours and textures. I enjoyed making and eating them, and I hope you will too. Most importantly, use this book as you see fit and in the way you will enjoy it best. Happy wrapping!

CHAPTER 1
BASES & BATTERS

FLOUR TORTILLAS

▲▲▲▲▲▲▲▲▲▲▲▲▲▲▲▲▲▲▲▲▲▲▲

The proper Mexican way is to use lard in tortilla dough, but many people opt for shortening nowadays. Although I'm more a fan of natural fats than man-made ones, the shortening here gives a wonderful texture to roll out. I also use baking powder, Tex-Mex style – a reflex action stemming from my roti-making roots. This is frowned upon by purists, but it makes the dough softer. This dough can be portioned and rolled to the desired size and thickness, as advised in the recipes, or to your taste. A silicone mat will allow you to roll out the dough really thinly.

> MAKES 4 LARGE TORTILLAS (22–24CM),
> 6 MEDIUM (19–20CM),
> 8 SMALL (18–19CM),
> 12 TAQUITO-SIZED (12CM)
> OR 4 THICK (19CM)
> (EASILY DOUBLED TO FEED LARGER NUMBERS)

200g plain flour, plus extra for dusting
scant ¼ tsp salt
1 tsp baking powder
25g vegetable shortening
100ml very hot water (or as needed)

Mix the flour, salt and baking powder together in a bowl. Add the shortening and water, which should be as hot as your hands can stand, and knead by hand for 2–3 minutes to make a supple and fairly soft dough. It will still be quite shaggy and rough-looking at this stage, but will become smooth when you re-knead it after resting. Shape into a ball and put it in the bowl. Cover with clingfilm or a damp cloth, and rest for at least 30 minutes, or up to 4 hours.

Once rested, knead the dough again lightly and divide into 4, 6, 8 or 12 pieces, shaping them into balls.

Heat a dry griddle or frying pan. Put a plate near the stove, place a spoon on it and cover with a tea towel. (Or have your tortilla keeper, lined with kitchen paper, at hand.)

On a lightly floured work surface, roll a large ball out to a thin neat circle about 25–27cm in diameter (22–23cm for medium, 20–22cm for small or 15–16cm for very small), dusting with flour as needed. Give it regular quarter turns as you roll, to keep it as round as you can and to discourage sticking. Make sure that the edges are thin.

[continues overleaf]

FLOUR TORTILLAS, cont.

Drape the tortilla over the rolling pin and transfer to the hot griddle; it will shrink a little and will rise slightly. Cook over a medium heat just until small bubbles appear on top and golden flecks appear on the base. Depending on your cooking utensil and heat source, this takes anything from several seconds to a minute or two. Flip it over and cook briefly on the second side. Press the top with a large spatula after you flip it over; this will encourage the tortilla to swell, making it lighter in texture. Don't overcook the tortillas or they will become crisp and hard. Transfer to the plate and fold the tea towel to cover it.

Cook the rest in the same way. Leave in the tea towel for a few minutes; the condensation will make them more pliable. Use as directed in the recipe.

These are delicious eaten fresh, but can also be warmed the next day, or frozen as soon as they are cool. If using a microwave, put them in layers of kitchen paper and heat very briefly, or they will become tough. For a conventional oven, stack and wrap in foil; put in a slow oven (about 150°C/ Gas Mark 2) just until warmed through.

VARIATIONS

Thick Tortillas
(see also Seasoned Roti Wrappers p.16)

Divide the dough into 4 pieces and shape into balls. Roll out to a diameter of about 22cm and cook as directed. This will give you 4 thick tortillas, about 19cm, ideal for Shawarma (see pp.56, 58), and souvlaki (p.61), etc.

Scandinavian Twist

Add 1 tsp granulated sugar, ¼ tsp ground aniseed and scant ¼ tsp ground cardamom to the dry ingredients when preparing the dough. Roll and cook as desired. Note that these are also excellent spread with butter, sprinkled with (brown) sugar and rolled up to eat with tea or coffee.

Tomato-Flavoured

Use scant 100ml very hot water and dissolve 1 tbsp tomato purée in it before proceeding in the usual way. If the dough feels very sticky, sprinkle a little flour over it. Lovely colour and flavour, and good with any recipe requiring tortillas, especially with cheese.

BASIC YEAST DOUGH

▲▲▲▲▲▲▲▲▲▲▲▲▲▲▲▲▲▲▲▲▲▲

This dough is suitable for very flat snacks such as pizza (see Middle Eastern Pizzas and Turnovers on p.78). It can be kneaded by hand, in a food processor fitted with a plastic kneading attachment or a mixer fitted with a dough hook. Plain flour makes the dough easier to roll out thinly, whereas strong flour can drive you to frustration by springing back every time you lift the rolling pin – and will have no added value in a thin pizza base.

MAKES 4 PIZZAS OR 8 TURNOVERS

250g plain flour
1½ tsp easy-blend dried yeast
½ tsp salt
1 tsp granulated sugar
2 tbsp olive oil
about 140ml lukewarm water

Combine the dry ingredients in a bowl. Add the liquids and knead well for several minutes. The dough should be soft but not sticky. Shape the dough into a ball and put it in a bowl. Cover with clingfilm, or a tea towel wrung out in hot water, and leave in a warm, draught-free place until doubled in size.

Use as directed in the recipe.

COCO BREAD & BUTTER FLAPS

There are two variations to this roll. In Jamaica, where it is a much-used 'holder' for jerk chicken, it is called 'coco bread' and the most popular shape is semi-circular. Some people give it a double fold to create a quarter circle with many pockets. That is the version I grew up with in Guyana, where it is known as a 'butter flap' and eaten as a snack in its own right. As well as Jerk Chicken (p.52), you can stuff sausages, kebabs and all kinds of salad in them.

MAKES 12

500g strong white flour, plus extra for dusting
2 tsp easy-blend dried yeast
2 tbsp granulated sugar
1 tsp salt
1 egg, well beaten
about 240ml lukewarm milk
75g butter, melted, plus 40–50g extra,
    plus extra for greasing

Put all of the ingredients except the extra melted butter in a large bowl and stir to incorporate. Use a heavy-duty mixer fitted with a dough hook to knead thoroughly until soft, smooth and supple. Alternatively, turn out onto a floured work surface or a silicone mat and knead. Bring together in a ball and return to the bowl. Cover with clingfilm and leave in a warm, draught-free place until doubled in size.

Grease 1 baking sheet for butter flaps and 2 for coco bread. Knock back the dough and knead lightly until smooth again. Divide into 12 portions and shape into balls. Cover loosely with clingfilm while you work.

Coco bread: Roll each ball out to a circle 15cm in diameter. Brush with some of the extra melted butter and fold over to form a semi-circle. Brush the tops with more melted butter and place on the baking sheets. Leave space for the rolls to expand.

Butter flaps: Roll out to 18cm and follow the steps above, giving them an extra fold to make a quarter circle. Brush the tops with the extra melted butter.

Cover loosely with clingfilm and leave in a warm, draught-free place until almost doubled in size.

Preheat the oven to 200°C/Gas Mark 6 and bake for about 12–15 minutes. Coco bread will cook faster as it is thinner. The tops should be light brown. Cool on a wire rack. They will be crisp on the outside when freshly baked, but will soften after a few hours. Keep for a day or two if well wrapped and can be frozen as soon as cool. Wrap individually and put in a freezer bag.

POCKET BREADS

▲▲▲▲▲▲▲▲▲▲▲▲▲▲▲▲▲▲▲▲▲▲▲▲▲▲▲▲

Granted, the best pitta or pocket breads are made in cavernous stone-floored, wood-fired Middle Eastern ovens, but you can make them at home too, without too much fuss.

MAKES 8 (ABOUT 15CM) (EASILY HALVED)

500g plain flour, plus extra for dusting
2 tsp easy-blend dried yeast
1 tsp salt
2 tsp granulated sugar
about 300ml lukewarm water
1 tbsp olive oil

Combine the dry ingredients in a bowl. Add the water, reserving about 1 tbsp, and mix with a spatula until all of the water has been absorbed. Add the oil, and the reserved water if needed, and knead well to make a soft but not sticky dough. You can do this by hand, or in a mixer fitted with a dough hook. Shape the dough into a ball and put it in a bowl. Cover with clingfilm or a damp tea towel, and leave in a warm, draught-free place until doubled in size.

Start preheating your oven in good time so that it really is 250°C/Gas Mark 9 by the time your dough is ready. If you have a pizza stone, put it in the oven too. If not, you can preheat a baking sheet just before needed.

Knock back the dough and knead briefly. Divide into 8 portions and shape into balls. Dust an area of work surface with flour, for the shaped breads. If you have a cold surface, such as marble, metal or stone, use a silicone mat or wooden board as insulation and dust this. Roll out a ball to a neat circle just over 15cm in diameter, dusting as needed. Place it on the floured surface and dust lightly with flour. Shape the rest in the same way.

Cover loosely with clingfilm and leave until puffed up to twice their original thickness.

Lift carefully and place slightly apart on the pizza stone, as quickly as possible so that you don't lose too much heat. Alternatively, put them on a hot baking sheet and slide them into the oven. They bake very fast, so you can do it in 2 batches if necessary and bake for 4–5 minutes. The stone will bake a little faster than the sheet. The breads will puff up nicely and develop their pockets. Note that the tops will remain light-coloured while the bases will brown a little.

Cool on a wire rack and keep in a plastic bag. They can also be frozen. Cut in half to serve, or make a slit along the side and stuff. Use for Shawarma (see pp.56, 58), Tandoori Chicken (see p.48), Jerk Chicken (see p.52), fish cakes, salad, whatever you like.

SEASONED ROTI WRAPPERS

▲▲▲▲▲▲▲▲▲▲▲▲▲▲▲▲▲▲▲▲▲▲▲

'Roti' is simply the Hindi word for bread, but to most people it means one of a marvellous assortment of griddled Indian flatbreads, thick, thin, flaky or chewy. This thick *roti* is ideal for things like meat skewers, Shawarma (see pp.56, 58), tandoori, etc.

MAKES 4 (ABOUT 20–22CM)

250g plain flour, plus extra for dusting
2 tsp baking powder
¼ tsp salt
1 tsp granulated sugar
1 spring onion, very finely chopped
1 tbsp very finely chopped flat-leaf parsley
   or coriander
¼ tsp chilli flakes
about 150ml lukewarm water
1 tbsp oil/ghee/butter,
   plus 2 tbsp extra ghee or
   knob of cold butter for brushing

Combine all the ingredients except for the extra fat to make a soft and supple dough. You can do this by hand, or in a mixer fitted with a dough hook. A food processor fitted with a kneading attachment makes quick work of it. Shape the dough into a ball and put it in a bowl. Cover with clingfilm and leave for 30–60 minutes.

Re-knead lightly and divide into 4 balls. Roll out each ball to a circle about 22–24cm in diameter, dusting well with flour as necessary on both sides.

Heat a dry griddle (tawa) or frying pan. When the pan is hot, reduce the heat. Slap a roti onto it; it will shrink a little and cook until there are a few bubbles on the top. Depending on your cooking utensil and heat source, this takes a minute or two. Flip the roti over and cook the other side briefly. Brush with extra ghee or rub with butter on both sides and keep wrapped in a tea towel until ready to eat. Cook the remaining roti in the same way.

TWO-FRIENDS WRAPPERS
< DOSTI ROTI OR '2-IN-1' >

These are popular in Guyana and Trinidad as a quicker alternative to the more time-consuming flaky parathas. 'Dost' means 'friend' in Hindi and the heartwarming name comes from the fact that they are rolled and cooked together in pairs and only separated afterwards. Eat warm or at room temperature, rolled around spicy meat or vegetables, or with a gravy dish such as curry.

MAKES 4 (EASILY DOUBLED)

200g plain flour, plus extra for dusting
⅛ tsp salt
1 tsp baking powder
¼ tsp granulated sugar
scant 120ml lukewarm water
 (or as needed)
1 tbsp sunflower or corn oil (or other
 neutral-tasting oil), plus about
 2 tbsp extra for brushing

Mix the dry ingredients together in a bowl. Add the water and 1 tbsp of oil and knead well, by hand or using the dough hook of the mixer, to make a smooth and fairly soft dough. Shape into a ball and put in the bowl. Cover with clingfilm or a damp cloth and leave for at least 30 minutes.

Re-knead the dough lightly and divide into 4 pieces, shaping them into balls.

Heat a dry griddle (tawa) or frying pan. Put a plate near the stove, invert a spoon on it and cover with a tea towel. (The spoon prevents moisture from building up.)

On a lightly floured work surface, flatten 2 balls into discs about 10cm in diameter. Brush one with oil and place the second one over this. Roll out the double-decker dough to form a circle about 24–25cm in diameter, dusting with flour as needed. Make sure that the edges are thin.

Slap the dough onto the hot tawa and brush the top with oil. After a minute or so, turn it over and brush the second side with oil. Cook briefly on both sides until small golden flecks appear. Overcooking will make them crisp and hard. Transfer to the plate and fold the tea towel to cover. As soon as they are cool enough to handle, ease the 2 rotis apart and replace in the tea towel. Make the rest in the same way.

To assemble your wrap, put a roti on a plate, with the light side facing upwards. Top with your choice of filling and roll into a tube or fold into a chunky parcel.

FLAKY PARATHAS

This is a variation of the Guyanese-style parathas I gave in my book *Warm Bread and Honey Cake*, rolled and shaped in a different way. They are wonderful for wraps and, if you bash them in a tea towel as soon as they come off the heat, they will be flakier. I often make a double batch and freeze half for a quick snack later.

MAKES 4

250g plain flour, plus extra for dredging
   and dusting
½ tsp granulated sugar
1 tsp baking powder
150ml lukewarm water, or as needed
2 tsp vegetable oil, plus extra for oiling
about 50g melted butter, ghee or
   neutral-tasting oil

Make a soft and pliable dough from the first 5 ingredients. Shape into a ball and put in a bowl. Cover with clingfilm or a damp cloth and leave at room temperature for at least 30 minutes.

Re-knead lightly and divide into 4 pieces. Oil a dinner plate. Roll out a piece of dough to a rectangle roughly 30 x 12cm. Brush with fat and dredge with flour. This is important or you won't get nice layers! Roll up Swiss-roll style and shape into a coil, tucking the end underneath. Put it on the oiled plate and cover loosely with clingfilm. Shape the rest in the same way, then leave for 30 minutes.

Put a second plate near to the stove. Invert a spoon on it and cover with a tea towel; have a second tea towel handy. Heat a dry griddle (*tawa*) or heavy-based frying pan.

Roll out a spiral to a circle about 22cm in diameter, dusting with flour as needed. Slap it onto the *tawa*. Brush the top lightly with fat, then after a minute or so, flip it over and brush the second side. Cook on both sides, pressing regularly with a spatula, until small golden flecks appear. Depending on your cooking utensil and heat source, this takes a minute or two. Overcooking will make them crisp and hard.

Transfer the paratha to the second tea towel and wrap loosely. Bash it with your fist a few times in various positions, or press with a crumpling movement, to loosen the layers. Transfer the paratha to the tea towel on the plate and fold to cover it. Cook the rest in the same way.

Eat fresh, preferably warm, or freeze for later, well wrapped. To reheat, wrap in a few layers of kitchen paper and reheat in short bursts in the microwave. If left in too long, they will become tough.

FRIED BREAD
< LÁNGOS OR BARA >

No visitor to Hungary and neighbouring countries will fail to see the popular street snack called *Lángos*. Similar to American Indian fried bread, it is sold from kiosks, and eaten brushed with garlic water and topped with the ubiquitous sour cream, and/or ham, cheese and the like. Eat hot or warm, with your choice of topping. Two tips worth sharing: sprinkle some dill over the sour cream; I like to add 1 tsp of aniseed to the dough for extra flavour. You could also use fennel, caraway or even cumin seeds. See below for spicy Caribbean *bara*.

> **MAKES 4 LÁNGOS AND 16 BARA**

250g plain flour
1¼ tsp easy-blend dried yeast
1 tsp granulated sugar
¼ tsp salt
180ml warm water
2 tsp neutral-tasting oil, plus extra for
    oiling and deep-frying

Combine the dry ingredients in a bowl. Add the water and stir with a spatula. Add the 2 tsp of oil and mix with a dough hook until smooth. Alternatively, beat with a wooden spatula until smooth. This is a soft and sticky dough, almost a batter. Bring the dough together with a scraper, cover with clingfilm or a damp cloth and leave in a warm, draught-free place until doubled in size.

Use the scraper to deflate the dough and to bring it all together again. Scrape it onto a silicone mat or a well-oiled plate. With oiled hands, pinch the dough into 4 pieces.

Line a plate with a tea towel and lay 2 sheets of kitchen paper on it. Heat the oil for deep-frying in a suitable pan to 185–190°C, or until a cube of bread browns in 30 seconds. Oiling your hands each time, take a portion of dough and flatten it between your palms. Slap, pull and stretch to make as large and thin a circle as you can, without tearing it. Lay it carefully in the oil and deep-fry until golden brown on one side. Turn over with tongs and cook on the second side. It should be golden brown and cooked through. Allow excess oil to drip back into the pan, then lay the bread on the plate, cover with 2 more sheets of kitchen paper and fold the towel closed. Cook the rest in the same way. Serve hot.

For **bara**, add an extra ⅛ tsp salt, ½ tsp turmeric, ½ tsp ground cumin and ½ tsp ground coriander to the dry ingredients and follow the instructions above. When you reach the shaping stage, pinch the dough into 16 pieces and flatten each into a thin disc about 9–10cm in diameter. Deep-fry in small batches. Use in pairs to sandwich curry, etc.

PASTRY FOR FRYING

This pastry allows itself to be rolled out very thinly, especially if you use a silicone mat, and is ideal for fried snacks such as Indonesian Pasties (see p.66), Curry Puffs (see below) and even Samosas (see p.71) (although it will give a softer finish). It is particularly delicious when eaten fresh and warm. And if you have never come across a curry puff: it's a fried turnover filled with a meat or chicken curry. They were a popular teatime treat in our house when I was growing up; I think my mother got the recipe for this mostly Malaysian snack from a foreign friend. If you'd like to try them, use the Guyanese chicken curry and this pastry, and shape and fry as described for Indonesian Pasties.

MAKES ENOUGH FOR 12 PASTIES/PUFFS OR 24 SAMOSAS

250g plain flour
generous ¼ tsp salt
60g butter, chilled and cubed
1 egg, well beaten
about 65ml lukewarm water, or as needed

Put the flour in a roomy bowl and stir in the salt. Rub in the butter with your fingertips until there are no lumps to be felt. Add the egg and water, and knead for about 3 minutes to make a firm but supple pastry. It will look fairly shaggy and rough-looking at this stage. Shape into a ball, put in the bowl, cover with clingfilm and leave at room temperature for 30 minutes.

Re-knead briefly until smooth and use as directed in the individual recipes.

CRÊPES

▲▲▲▲▲▲▲▲▲▲▲▲▲▲▲▲▲▲▲▲▲▲▲

Use these on their own with a squeeze of lemon juice and a sprinkle of icing sugar, or to compose other desserts. Sparkling water or soda water gives an airier texture than milk alone, but both are delicious. You can leave them pale and pliable or cook them a little longer to brown them a little, which adds flavour. Too crisp and they will be harder to fold. Note that the first is not usually as good-looking as the rest and the last may be a bit scanty and lacy. These are for the cook. This recipe makes enough for 10–12 x 23–24cm crêpes using a 50ml ladle.

MAKES ABOUT 600ML BATTER

150g plain flour
⅛ tsp salt
2 tsp granulated sugar
2 eggs, well beaten
½ tsp vanilla extract
large pinch of grated lemon or orange zest
    (optional)
200ml milk, plus 200ml sparkling mineral
    water or soda water, or 400ml milk
melted butter or neutral-tasting oil,
    for brushing

Sift the flour into a bowl and add the salt and sugar. Add the beaten eggs, vanilla, citrus zest and 200ml milk, and whisk to make a thick batter. Whisk in the mineral or soda water (or the rest of the milk) a little at a time, to make the batter more fluid. The batter will froth up as you add the mineral water. Whisk until smooth, then cover with clingfilm and leave at cool room temperature for about 15–30 minutes.

When ready to cook, heat a 23–24cm non-stick pan and brush lightly with melted butter or oil. Give the batter a good stir and use a small 50ml ladle to dip out a portion of batter. Hold the pan in one hand, off the heat, and pour into the centre of the pan, swirling the pan as you pour, to spread the batter quickly before it starts to set. Any small holes can be repaired with a few drops of batter. Cook over a medium heat until the edges start to colour. As soon as the base is cooked, flip the crêpe over gently without damaging it and cook briefly on the other side. Transfer to a plate and keep warm while you cook the rest. Stir the batter every time before dipping, and brush the pan with butter or oil for each crêpe.

CHAPTER 2
WRAPS & ROLLS

FRESH SPRING ROLLS

▲▲▲▲▲▲▲▲▲▲▲▲▲▲▲▲▲▲▲▲▲

These are called 'fresh lumpia' in the Philippines. Unlike the better known Indonesian and Chinese spring rolls, this version is not fried, but made from thin pancakes wrapped around a variety of fillings. Assemble them and serve immediately, or put everything on the table and let everyone compose their own. It makes a lovely party piece and is an excellent ice-breaker as people pass dishes to their neighbours. Choose vegetables that will offer a variety of textures, soft and crunchy, as suggested below. The components can be prepared in advance and the sauce can even be made the day before. Serve at room temperature. This recipe makes 8 rolls from 20cm pancakes (make smaller pancakes if you want more rolls).

MAKES 8

FILLING
1 tbsp groundnut or sunflower oil
2 garlic cloves, crushed
100g shiitake mushrooms, sliced ½cm thick
100g mangetout, cut into ½cm strips
100g carrot, cut into matchsticks
125g bean sprouts
1 tbsp Japanese-style soy sauce

SAUCE
2 tbsp cornflour
200ml water
2 tbsp brown sugar
2 tbsp Japanese-style soy sauce
1½–2 tsp good fruity vinegar,
   such as white balsamic or cider
1 garlic clove, crushed

WRAPPERS
125g plain flour
25g cornflour
1 egg
2 tsp neutral-tasting oil
275ml water
groundnut or sunflower oil, for cooking

TOPPINGS
8 fairly large flexible lettuce leaves,
   such as butter lettuce
red and green chillies, thinly sliced
3 spring onions, thinly sliced
250–300g skinless chicken breast,
   cooked and shredded
about 24 medium prawns,
   peeled and cooked
75g roasted peanuts, crushed or
   finely chopped

For the filling, heat the oil in a wok or large, heavy-based frying pan, add the garlic and stir-fry for 30 seconds before adding the mushrooms. Keep on moving them around with a spatula and as soon as they have absorbed the oil, add the mangetout and carrot matchsticks. Stir-fry briefly until the mangetout is barely cooked, then add the bean sprouts and soy sauce, and stir-fry for a minute or so more. The vegetables should remain quite crisp. Set aside.

For the sauce, dissolve the cornflour in about 5 tbsp of the water. Put the remaining water into a small pan and add the sugar and soy sauce. Place it over a medium heat and stir to dissolve the sugar. When the liquid is very hot, give the cornflour mixture a good stir and pour it into the pan, stirring continuously. Let it come to the boil, reducing the heat if necessary, still stirring gently all the time. It will change from a dark coffee colour to a darker brown as it thickens. Remove from the heat and stir in the vinegar to taste. Add the garlic and set aside until needed. This can be done the day before and the sauce can be kept in a screw-topped jar in the fridge. The sauce should be thick but you should be able to drizzle it over the filling. If it has thickened too much, stir in a little hot water, 1 tsp at a time, until you get the desired consistency.

The wrappers are very easy to mix using a stick blender or food processor. Simply blitz all of the ingredients until you get a smooth batter. If you are doing it by hand, combine the dry ingredients in a bowl. Beat the egg well and mix it with the water and oil. Pour this over the flour mixture and whisk until smooth. Set aside for 15 minutes or until needed.

Heat a 20cm non-stick pan and brush lightly with oil. Reduce the heat to medium. Give the batter a good stir and pour a 50ml ladleful into the centre of the pan. Swirl the pan to allow the batter to spread and coat the base of the pan. Fill in any empty spaces with a few drops of batter. As soon as the top of the pancake has dried and the edge curls a little, loosen it carefully and flip it over, transferring it to a plate after 20–30 seconds. Don't overcook them. You want barely cooked, pliable pancakes, not crisp ones. Cook the rest in the same way, stirring the batter and oiling the pan before each pancake. Add each new one to the pile on the plate. Set aside until ready to serve.

Serve at room temperature. Arrange all of the components on the table and give each person a plate. Lay a pancake on each plate. Put a lettuce leaf in the centre of each pancake. You really need this lettuce leaf or all the filling will burst through the delicate pancake! Top with a helping of vegetables, shredded chicken and a few prawns. Drizzle over some of the sauce and sprinkle on a few peanuts, chillies and spring onions. Fold the bottom part over to cover part of the filling, then fold in the sides to form a neat but chunky roll.

KOREAN BEEF BUNDLES
< BULGOGI >

Literally 'fire meat', *bulgogi* is a popular street food in Korea. Paper-thin slices of sweetish flash-grilled beef are laid on lettuce leaves and topped with spicy *kimchi* (a fermented pickle) and similar condiments. Some people add a little rice or vermicelli to make a more substantial package. I use rice here and accompany it with a *Kimchi*-style Cucumber Pickle (see p.125). Note that both meat and pickle need to marinate overnight. The meat is reputedly always of the highest quality possible, but nobody stops to check that vendors are telling the truth, and local marinating techniques (including nashi pear pulp) can work wonders on more ordinary meat. Having said that, do use good-quality steak for this recipe. You will need about 175g (dry weight) of jasmine rice for this recipe.

SERVES ABOUT 4 AS A SNACK

300g good steak, in a thick piece
2 garlic cloves, crushed
1 medium white onion, grated to pulp
1 spring onion, very thinly sliced
1 tbsp granulated sugar
1 tbsp sesame oil
3 tbsp Japanese-style soy sauce

Slice the steak as thinly as you can and put it in a bowl with a well-fitting cover. Mix the remaining ingredients together and use your hands to rub the marinade into the meat, separating the pieces as you work. Cover and refrigerate overnight.

Next day, bring the meat to room temperature. Heat a heavy-based frying pan or stovetop grill pan until very hot and lay the steak slices flat in the pan. Cook in batches, keeping them slightly pink on the inside or cooking them through if you prefer. The sugar will caramelise and brown nicely, so clean the pan between batches.

To serve, take a flexible lettuce leaf, such as butter lettuce, top with a dollop of cooked jasmine rice, some meat and *Kimchi*-style Cucumber Pickle (see p.125) to taste. Don't overload, or the leaf will break. Roll up or fold to enclose the filling and enjoy. It doesn't make for elegant eating, but your companions will be too busy to see you.

CRYSTAL OR SUMMER ROLLS

▲▲▲▲▲▲▲▲▲▲▲▲▲▲▲▲▲▲▲▲▲▲▲▲▲

Banh trang, sheets of rice wafers, always look so spectacular that you would think that they are difficult to work with. Nothing is further from the truth. They only need moistening and then you can fill them with all kinds of tasty things. A traditional Vietnamese filling is given here, but see p.32 for a quick and crunchy variation. You can also scatter a few chopped peanuts on the filling before rolling up.

MAKES 8

8 x 22cm sheets of Vietnamese rice wafers
8 flexible lettuce leaves, such as butter
  lettuce
16 mint leaves
16 coriander sprigs
about 1.5 litres water
125g bean sprouts
100g thin rice noodles (dry weight)
24 medium cooked prawns
handful of chopped peanuts (optional)

Arrange the stack of rice wafers, lettuce, mint and coriander on the work surface. Bring the water to the boil in a large pan. Throw in the bean sprouts and turn off the heat after 1 minute. Use a slotted spoon to transfer the bean sprouts to a colander, rinse with cold water and drain. Set aside with the other waiting ingredients.

Use the water in the pan to prepare the rice noodles according to the manufacturer's instructions. Pull the noodles apart to make 8 portions. Remove the prawns from the fridge.

Take a large shallow bowl and fill it with boiling water. Have a platter standing by. Lay a sheet of clingfilm on the work surface. Take a rice wafer, dip it in the very hot water and lay it on the clingfilm. At this stage, it will be pliable, but will still be clear-coloured. Lay 3 prawns vertically along the centre then put a lettuce leaf on top. Lay a line of noodles and top with 2 mint leaves and 2 coriander sprigs, followed by the bean sprouts. Roll up tightly, tucking in the 2 ends when you get to the filling, to make a neat roll.

Lay the rolls on a platter (or individual plates if you prefer), so that the prawns are on top. Make sure that they don't touch, or the moisture will make them stick. Serve as soon as possible after filling. Serve with *Nuoc Cham* (see p.129) dipping sauce and/or Simple Peanut Sauce (see p.130).

CRUNCHY & QUICK CRYSTAL ROLLS

Here is a quick and easy Crystal Roll variation, using surimi crab sticks. If your budget can bear it, crab (proper crabmeat, not the canned stuff) is absolutely wonderful. Smoked salmon is another option.

MAKES 8

8 x 22cm sheets of Vietnamese rice wafers

8 flexible lettuce leaves,
    such as butter lettuce

½ large cucumber, cut into thin matchsticks

1 large carrot, cut into thin matchsticks

16 surimi crab sticks

1 avocado, peeled, stoned and
    cut into 16 slices

16 mint leaves

16 dill sprigs

Arrange the stack of rice wafers, and the filling ingredients on the work surface.

Take a large shallow bowl and fill it with boiling water. Have a platter standing by. Lay a sheet of clingfilm on the work surface. Take a rice wafer, dip it in the very hot water and lay it on the clingfilm. At this stage, it will be pliable, but will still be clear-coloured. Place a lettuce leaf in the centre. Scatter on an eighth of the cucumber and carrot matchsticks. Arrange 2 surimi crab sticks in a line along the middle. Top with 2 avocado slices, 2 mint leaves and 2 dill sprigs. (Or, for a pretty effect, lay the herbs on the wrapper just beyond the lettuce leaf, so you can see them through the wrapper.) Roll up tightly, tucking in the 2 ends, to make a neat roll.

Lay the rolls on a platter (or individual plates if you prefer), making sure that they don't touch, or the moisture will make them stick. Serve as soon as possible with *Nuoc Cham* (see p.129) dipping sauce and/or Simple Peanut Sauce (see p.130).

CHICKEN FAJITAS

Picture a group of hungry Mexican cowboys sizzling meat in a cast-iron frying pan over a smoky campfire and then piling it with a whole load of condiments into a freshly cooked flour tortilla. It would have been skirt steak, the bit between the brisket and flank steak. Mexican cowboys working on the American side of the border in the early to mid-twentieth century were given this and other irregular cuts when beef was butchered on the ranch. Chicken and pork are now popular – and cheaper – options for this Tex-Mex snack. Cook the meat and peppers on the stove or on the barbecue and put them with the accompaniments on the table for diners to assemble their own fajitas. Marinate overnight for the best flavour.

ENOUGH TO FILL 4–6 LARGE FLOUR TORTILLAS

2 skinless, boneless chicken breasts (400g)
1–2 garlic cloves, crushed
1 tsp dried oregano
¾ tsp ground cumin
¼ tsp ground allspice
¼–½ tsp ground chilli
salt, to taste
juice of ½ lime
1 tbsp olive oil
about 2 tbsp groundnut or sunflower oil
1 small red pepper, sliced lengthways into strips 5mm wide
1 small green pepper, sliced lengthways into strips 5mm wide
1 large white onion, sliced lengthways into strips 5mm wide

Remove the tenderloin from the breasts, if present, then slice each chicken breast horizontally into 2 evenly sized pieces. Rub the chicken with the garlic, oregano, spices, generous ¼ tsp salt and the lime juice, then rub in the olive oil. Put in a non-reactive container with a well-fitting lid and chill for at least 1 hour, or preferably overnight.

Heat a frying pan or stovetop grill pan and cook the chicken until well done. Slice into 5mm pieces when ready to serve.

Meanwhile, heat the groundnut oil in a wok or frying pan and stir-fry the peppers and onions so that the peppers retain some bite. Sprinkle with a little salt. If you only have one pan/burner available, cook the chicken first and keep it warm (unsliced) in foil while you cook the vegetables.

Lay a warm Flour Tortilla (see p.10) on a plate and top with the chicken, vegetables and your choice of grated cheese, sour cream, Salsa Fresca (p.112), Cooked Salsa (p.112), Mango Salsa (p.120), Guacamole (p.114) and sliced avocado. I find cheese essential and the rest optional. Fold and enjoy.

BURRITOS & CHIMICHANGAS

▲▲▲▲▲▲▲▲▲▲▲▲▲▲▲▲▲▲▲▲▲▲▲▲▲▲▲▲▲

Burrito, diminutive of *burro*, means 'small donkey' and this snack supposedly got its name from its resemblance to said creature's ears. True or not, it is a delicious combination of wonderful Mexican flavours and you can choose to add or remove components to your heart's desire. Nicely parcelled and deep-fried, a burrito becomes a chimichanga. You will need about 4 large (24cm) tortillas and 75–100g (dry weight) of rice for this recipe.

MAKES 4

1–2 tbsp olive oil
1 medium onion, finely chopped
2 garlic cloves, crushed
300g lean minced beef
150g canned chopped tomatoes
½ tsp chilli powder, or to taste
¾ tsp ground cumin
1 tsp dried oregano
generous ¼ tsp salt or to taste

Heat the oil in a heavy-based pan, add the onion and garlic, and fry until softened. Add the mince and stir to break it up. Cook for a minute or two before adding the tomatoes and seasonings. Stir well, reduce the heat and cover the pan. Simmer for about 20 minutes, adding a little water, if needed, to prevent it catching on the base of the pan. This filling can be prepared ahead and reheated when you assemble the burritos.

Take a warm Flour Tortilla (p.10). Place a portion of Refried Beans (p.131) vertically along the middle, leaving about 3cm free at the top and bottom. (Or you can take the filling all the way up to the top if,

like me, you don't see the need to fold the top and bite it off next minute. And this way it looks more like a donkey's ear.) Put a serving of cooked rice on top, followed by a serving of meat. Sprinkle some grated cheese on top of this and drizzle with sour cream, if liked. Guacamole or Avocado Salad (see p.114) can go on top, or be served on the side. Fold over the bottom flap and fold the left and right side inwards to make a neat parcel. Wrap the bottom half of the burrito in foil, so you can eat in peace without having sauce drip down and things fall out.

Chimichanga: Put the Refried Beans, rice and meat in the centre of the tortilla and fold 2 sides inwards, overlapping over the filling. Secure with a cocktail stick. Fold the 2 ends inwards and secure each separately, to make a squarish parcel. Heat enough oil for deep-frying in a suitable pan to 180–185°C/350–365°F or until a cube of bread browns in 30 seconds and deep-fry until crisp and golden. Drain on kitchen paper and serve with condiments to taste.

SHREDDED BEEF TACOS

▲▲▲▲▲▲▲▲▲▲▲▲▲▲▲▲▲▲▲▲▲▲▲▲▲▲

These are made with soft flour tortillas and are far removed from the ones made with crisp ready-made 'U'-shaped taco shells from the supermarket. The meat for the filling has to be simmered for a few hours until tender, but don't let this put you off. It is actually very convenient. It needs no watching and can be cooked in advance so that it will be ready to fry with the spices whenever you like. (And you'll have a nice little bowl of stock left.) As they are usually folded into half moons, I find a medium-sized (about 18cm) tortilla handy to fill and eat, but feel free to use smaller or larger tortillas, as you like. Make the tortillas and accompaniments while cooking the meat.

MAKES 8

500g stewing steak, cut into 2–3cm chunks
1 bay leaf
2–3 cloves
½ tsp salt
500ml water
2 tbsp olive oil
1 large white onion, thinly sliced
2 garlic cloves, crushed
2 tsp dried oregano
1 tsp ground cumin
¼–½ tsp chilli powder
salt as needed

Put the steak into a pan with the bay leaf, cloves, salt and water. Cover and bring to the boil, skimming the scum off the surface. Reduce the heat, cover and simmer for a few hours until the meat is very tender. Use as soon as it can be handled or leave it in the cooking liquid until you need it, refrigerating if necessary. When ready to use the meat, drain the liquid and reserve

for another use, such as for Refried Beans (see p.131), soup, rice, etc. and shred the cooked beef.

Heat the oil in a non-stick pan, add the onion and garlic, and cook until softened. Add the shredded beef and the remaining ingredients and stir-fry until the meat is hot and everything is well combined. Taste for salt and add if needed.

Put a warm tortilla on a plate. Use Cooked Salsa or Salsa Fresca (see p.112). If using Cooked Salsa, start with that. Spread some on one half of the tortilla, followed by a portion of beef. Put some shredded cheese on top, if liked, then top with Guacamole (see p.114). For Salsa Fresca (p.112), start with the Guacamole and end with the Salsa Fresca. Add some finely shredded lettuce and/or sour cream, if liked. Fold in half and serve immediately. Keep napkins handy.

TAQUITOS

▲▲▲▲▲▲▲▲▲▲▲▲▲▲▲▲▲▲▲▲▲▲

Literally 'little tacos', these small crisp rolls are a variation of the slimmer and more elegant *flautas* (flutes) made in Mexico. They make a delicious appetiser, dipped in sour cream. These make 12 generously filled, chunky taquitos or 18 slimmer, more elegant ones.

MAKES 12–18

12–18 small (12cm) Flour Tortillas (see p.10)
1 recipe meat filling for Burritos (see p.34)
neutral-tasting oil, for shallow or
   deep-frying, or brushing

Make and cook the tortillas as directed on p.10.

Put a horizontal line of meat filling slightly below the centre of a tortilla, leaving about 2cm free at the sides. Roll up neatly and secure with a cocktail stick.

They can now be brushed with oil (for a crisper finish) or left plain, and baked for 15–20 minutes in an oven preheated to 200°C/Gas Mark 6. Or they can be shallow fried in 1–2cm oil, turning once so that both sides crisp up. Alternatively, fold the ends in to completely enclose the filling and heat enough oil for deep-frying in a suitable pan to 180–185°C/350–365°F, or until a cube of bread browns in 30 seconds. Deep-fry in batches until crisp and golden, then drain on kitchen paper.

Serve hot with sour cream.

QUESADILLAS

The word translates more or less as 'little cheesy things' and that is what this simple Mexican treat is all about: softly melted cheese with a few add-ins, sandwiched between two crisply toasted tortillas. It is a tasty snack, made in minutes from a few leftover tortillas. I was recently served a delicious version at a barbecue: hard goat's cheese with slivers of red onion and ribbons of courgette (pared with a potato peeler). Or try a blue-veined cheese, crumbled and mixed with finely chopped celery and walnuts. Or even Cheddar, rocket and pickle. The most important things are to use a generous amount of cheese with good melting properties, and not to overload the quesadilla with add-ins. Keep it simple. I'll let you work out your own favourite combinations. This recipe makes one medium-sized quesadilla, which is handier to cook and turn whole. Larger ones can be folded to make half-moons.

MAKES 1 (ABOUT 18CM)

2 x 18cm Flour Tortillas (see p.10)
at least 50g shredded tasty cheese,
   such as Cheddar, Gruyère or Gouda
1 spring onion, very thinly sliced
½–1 pickled jalapeño, thinly sliced and/or
   a few pitted black olives, sliced

Make and cook the tortillas as directed on p.10.

Lay a tortilla on your work surface and sprinkle half the cheese over it. Scatter on your toppings and sprinkle on the rest of the cheese. The cheese is your 'glue', so don't go for a shortcut and use it all on the bottom! Top with the second tortilla.

Heat a stovetop grill pan or ordinary frying pan, or fire up your barbecue. A panini grill is ideal, if you happen to have one, as it cooks both sides at once. Lay the quesadilla carefully in the dry pan, or on the barbecue and toast until the base is crisp. Carefully turn over with a large spatula and allow to crisp on the second side. Cut into wedges and eat warm, optionally with Guacamole (see p.114) or a salsa.

PHILLY CHEESE STEAK WRAPS

Philadelphia's pride and joy is a mighty mouthful: a long roll filled with thinly sliced steak, fried onion and pepper and nicely melting cheese. This version is housed in flour tortillas and one will make a satisfyingly large snack or even light meal if served with a salad, or steamed vegetables, with a vinaigrette or your favourite dressing. If you're eating with children, you can make smaller tortillas with part of the dough and portion the filling accordingly. Note that the real Philly steak is sliced paper thin. Many people freeze it partially first, to make it easier to slice thinly. Whatever method you choose, keep it thin.

MAKES 4

300g good-quality steak, in a thick piece
1½–2 tbsp neutral-tasting oil for cooking,
    or as needed
1 red pepper, sliced into strips
    about 5mm wide
1 large onion, sliced into strips
    about 5mm wide
salt and freshly ground black pepper
4 large Flour Tortillas (see p.10), warmed
80–100g tasty Cheddar or Gouda,
    coarsely shredded

Slice the steak thinly and set aside. Heat the oil in a wok or frying pan, add the sliced pepper and onion, and season with salt and pepper. Stir-fry until the onion takes on some colour and is just cooked through. Remove from the pan and keep warm.

Meanwhile, heat a stovetop grill pan and spread out the sliced steak to cook, turning as needed until seared or cooked to your liking. If you have managed to slice it really thinly, you may need to cook it in a few batches. Season with salt and pepper as needed.

Spread out the warm tortillas on plates and put a portion of onion and pepper along the middle. Top with a portion of steak and, finally, sprinkle on the shredded cheese. Roll up and serve immediately.

TERIYAKI-STYLE SALMON

Although this is something that is normally eaten with rice, it goes well with wraps too. If you prefer to make more of a meal of it, add a few handfuls of crisply cooked vegetables such as pak choy, bean sprouts or mangetout, or even asparagus or Tenderstem broccoli. Toss the vegetables in a little soy sauce, sesame oil and garlic before adding, to maximise flavour.

MAKES 4

600g skinless salmon fillet

2 spring onions, chopped

2 large garlic cloves, crushed

1 red chilli, sliced

small thumb-sized piece of fresh ginger, peeled and sliced

2 tbsp Japanese-style soy sauce

1 tbsp rice vinegar

1 tsp granulated sugar

1 tbsp cornflour

about 2 tbsp groundnut or corn oil, for cooking

4 large Flour Tortillas or *Dosti Roti* (see p.10 and p.18)

few handfuls of blanched or stir-fried vegetables tossed in soy sauce, sesame oil and garlic (optional)

Cut the salmon into 2cm chunks, put in a non-reactive bowl and set aside. Put the spring onions, garlic, chilli and ginger in a small blender/food processor, add the remaining ingredients (except the oil) and blitz to a paste. If you don't have a suitable blender/food processor, slice the ingredients very thinly and pound thoroughly with a mortar and pestle before adding the rest and pounding to a liquidish paste. Stir this marinade into the salmon and leave for 15–20 minutes, or even overnight. If the latter, put it in a sealed container in the fridge.

Heat the oil in a non-stick frying pan and cook the salmon until slightly pink in the middle or just cooked through. Use a flexible spatula to turn the pieces in the pan, to prevent the fish from breaking up.

Arrange along the centre of the wraps. Top optionally with the vegetables and roll up to eat.

MINCED CHICKEN SATAYS
< SATAY LILIT AYAM >

▲▲▲▲▲▲▲▲▲▲▲▲▲▲▲▲▲▲▲▲▲▲▲▲▲▲▲▲▲▲

As well as the more usual satays made from cubed meat, the Balinese are fond of using minced meat and fish to make tasty variations. There are many ways to use this recipe, so choose the one that suits you best. Lemongrass stalks give an attractive presentation. However, unless you are blessed with very fresh stalks, they will not provide as much aroma as you might expect from such an expensive ingredient. Flat bamboo or metal skewers are practical as the meat will slide around on a regular skewer. But be sure that all will fit flat in the pan or on the griddle. Failing all else, simply make patties that can be cooked in any pan.

MAKES 8

8 trimmed and lightly bruised lemongrass
   stalks or 8 flat skewers (see above)
1 lemongrass stalk, trimmed and sliced
2 spring onions, roughly chopped
1 bird's-eye or other chilli
2.5cm piece of fresh ginger, peeled
   and sliced
1 large garlic clove, sliced
½ tsp turmeric
½ tsp ground coriander
½ tsp ground cumin
3 tbsp desiccated coconut
1 tsp palm or soft brown sugar
1 tbsp soy sauce (*kecap manis* or
   Japanese style)
¼ tsp salt, or to taste
350g skinless, boneless chicken breast,
   cut into small chunks
butter, for greasing (optional)
groundnut or corn oil, for cooking

If using bamboo skewers, soak them in for a few hours to delay charring. Put the sliced lemongrass and other flavourings in a food processor and blitz until fine. Add the chicken and pulse until paste-like. Chill for at least 30 minutes, or up to several hours.

Divide the chicken mixture into 8 portions and mould each portion into a 10cm 'sausage' around the thick part of a lemongrass stalk (cut to fit the cooking utensil) or around a skewer. Alternatively, make elongated patties. Lay on a greased plate or on a piece of clingfilm on the work surface. Shape the rest in the same way.

Heat a few tsp of oil in a heavy-based seasoned frying pan, or lightly brush a non-stick surface. Cook the chicken on all sides until completely cooked through. Serve 2 per portion, warm or at room temperature, with Flour Tortillas (p.10), Seasoned Roti Wrappers (p.16) or even Coco Bread (p.12), accompanied by Peanut Sauce (p.130) and Cucumber Chutney (p.121), or sliced or diced cucumber tossed in salt and vinegar.

TANDOORI-STYLE CHICKEN SKEWERS

▲▲▲▲▲▲▲▲▲▲▲▲▲▲▲▲▲▲▲▲▲▲▲▲▲▲▲▲

The ferocious heat of a traditional tandoor oven sears and cooks foods in record time, tingeing them with a lovely wood-smoke flavour at the same time. Tandoori chicken and naan are two well-known examples. Home cooks can make a simple version of the chicken under the grill or on the barbecue. Instead of naan, pair it with Seasoned Roti Wrappers (p.16), Parathas (p.20) or bara made to the size of Lángos (p.21). I think they are best plain in the wrap, but you can add a few strips of roasted pepper if you like, and serve something like Hot, Sweet & Sour Fruit Salad (p.116) or Mango Salsa (p.120) on the side. Note that the chicken should be marinated overnight.

MAKES 8

400g skinless, boneless chicken breast, cut into small chunks (2–2.5cm)
Seasoned Roti Wrappers (see p.16) or Parathas (see p.20)

MARINADE
4 tbsp full-fat thick Greek-style yogurt
2 tsp ground cumin
1½ tsp ground coriander
½ tsp ground paprika
¼–½ tsp chilli powder
¼ tsp ground cinnamon
¼ tsp ground allspice
½ tsp salt, or to taste
small thumb of fresh ginger, peeled and grated
2 garlic cloves, crushed
2 tsp lime juice

If using bamboo skewers, soak them in water for a few hours to delay charring.

Combine the marinade ingredients and mix in the chicken. Put in a well-sealed container and chill overnight.

Next day, preheat the grill to high or fire up a barbecue. Thread the chicken pieces onto the skewers and cook them under the hot grill or on the barbecue until completely cooked through. If using the grill, make sure that the skewers are on a rack slightly raised from the base, so that the chicken does not lie in the liquid that it will give off.

Put 2 skewers onto each wrapper and fold over. Press the wrap with one hand and ease off the skewers with the other.

GUYANESE CHICKEN CURRY

▲▲▲▲▲▲▲▲▲▲▲▲▲▲▲▲▲▲▲▲▲▲▲

There is not a house in Guyana where this curry is not eaten – nor in neighbouring Trinidad and Surinam, for that matter. Indian indentured labourers who came to work on the sugar plantations after the abolition of slavery brought their food with them. Over time, it became mainstream and took on an identity of its own, and Indian and Indo-Caribbean dishes with similar names can be quite different. It was a case of making do with the ingredients that were available locally, as this curry illustrates. The labourers were given weekly rations, which included pre-mixed masala and curry powder, and the Indo-Caribbean curry was born. Curry wrapped in a *roti* is Trinidadian 'fast' food. As a child, I always looked forward to stopping at a roadside stall with Uncle Mootee to pick up one of these treats.

> **MAKES ENOUGH TO FILL 6–8 DOSTI ROTIS**
> **(MAKE A DOUBLE BATCH OF ROTI)**

1 generous tbsp (Madras) curry powder

1 tsp garam masala

150ml warm water, plus about 1 tbsp water

2 tbsp groundnut or corn oil

1 medium onion, finely chopped

2 garlic cloves, crushed

500g boneless chicken breast, cut into small
   bite-sized pieces

1 large potato, peeled and diced
   (sugar-cube size)

about ¾ tsp salt, or to taste

6–8 *Dosti Rotis* (see p.18)

Put the curry powder and garam masala into a small teacup and add the 1 tbsp water. Mix to make a paste, adding a little more water if necessary.

Heat the oil in a wok or heavy-based pan, add the onion and fry for a minute or two before adding the garlic. Continue to fry for another 2 minutes, or until the onion is almost cooked through. Add the curry paste and stir vigorously for a few seconds. It will stick to the base. Throw in the chicken and stir-fry briefly, so that most of the meat is seared. Don't wait too long, or the curry powder will burn. Reduce the heat and pour in the 150ml warm water. Stir well and scrape the base of the pan to loosen the curry powder that has caught. Add the potatoes and salt, and simmer until the chicken and potatoes are cooked through, tender, and only a little sauce is left coating the base of the pan. If the liquid evaporates too fast, add 1 extra tbsp water as needed. Taste and add more salt if necessary.

Spoon out generously into 6–8 *rotis*, fold and enjoy.

PARATHA EGG SANDWICH

▲▲▲▲▲▲▲▲▲▲▲▲▲▲▲▲▲▲▲▲▲

Also known as 'Indian egg rolls', these can be made in a number of ways. Some recipes involve stuffing a cooked filling into raw dough before cooking; others require you to half-cook a triangular pocket paratha and to pour the liquid filling in before cooking completely. Yet other variations ask you to partially cook the omelette before sticking the cooked paratha on top and cooking it further. All perfectly tasty in their own way, but all designed to overcook the paratha and make it hard instead of nice and flaky. A Southern Indian friend advised me to cook the two separately, as many street vendors do, and I find this the best option.

The spicing of the omelettes is a matter of personal taste, and Northern Indian versions often use garam masala and ginger as well. Be generous with the salt and spices as the paratha itself is quite bland.

MAKES 4

4 Parathas (see p.20)
4 eggs
salt to taste
turmeric to taste
ground cumin to taste
freshly ground black pepper
2–4 green chillies, thinly sliced
1 fairly large onion, finely chopped
small handful of coriander leaves,
   roughly chopped
neutral-tasting oil, for cooking

Make the Parathas and keep them warm folded in the tea towel while you prepare the omelettes.

In a small bowl, whisk an egg with salt to taste (on the generous side), 1/8–1/4 tsp each of turmeric and cumin and a good grind of black pepper. Mix in a quarter of the chilli, onion and coriander leaves. Heat some oil in a (non-stick) frying pan and pour in the egg mixture, shaking the pan to spread it. Cook until set and lightly browned on the base, then flip over and brown lightly on the second side. If you want to serve all 4 at once, keep the omelette warm and cook the rest. As soon as the last omelette is cooked, slide it out onto a warmed paratha, roll up and eat warm.

JERK CHICKEN

▲▲▲▲▲▲▲▲▲▲▲▲▲▲▲▲▲▲▲▲

In Jamaica, they often use a few twigs and branches from the allspice (pimento) tree to add its typical fragrance to jerk barbecues, but even without them, you can make good jerk chicken at home. It must be fiery to be 'authentic'. Scotch bonnet chillies give the best flavour and the most heat, but you can use less if preferred. Instructions follow for roasting, but it can also be cooked on a barbecue. Start marinading at least 24 hours in advance.

**FILLS 12 COCO BREAD ROLLS OR
8 LARGE FLOUR TORTILLAS (EASILY HALVED)**

1 x 1.5kg chicken on the bone
   or 1.2kg boneless thighs
12 Coco Bread rolls (see p.12) or
   8 large Flour Tortillas (see p.10)

JERK MARINADE
3 spring onions, trimmed and chopped
1 Scotch bonnet chilli or larger amount of
   milder chillies, deseeded
4 garlic cloves, sliced
thumb-sized piece of fresh ginger, peeled
   and sliced
1 tbsp dried thyme
1 tsp ground allspice
1 heaped tsp brown sugar
1 tbsp vegetable oil
3 tbsp Japanese-style soy sauce
3 tbsp light-coloured vinegar
½ tsp salt, or to taste

Put all of the marinade ingredients in a food processor and process to a paste. Cut the whole chicken into medium-sized pieces. Drumsticks can be left as they are. Each thigh should be cut in half and each side of breast quartered. Leave the wings whole, but detach them from the breast. Take a sharp knife and pierce each chicken piece in at least 3 places, going down to the bone and widening the hole slightly. This is not necessary if using boneless thighs. Put in a large bowl and pour on the marinade. (Wear gloves if your hands are not chilli-proof!) Rub the marinade well in, taking care to get some into all the crevices. Put in a covered glass dish (or use a large zipper freezer bag) and chill for 24–48 hours. The longer you leave it, the more flavourful it will be. When you are ready to cook, bring the chicken to room temperature.

Preheat the oven to 180°C/Gas Mark 4. Arrange the chicken in a large roasting tin and cook for 25–30 minutes for boneless thighs and 40–45 minutes for whole chicken pieces, or until well cooked through. If you find that the chicken is browning too fast, cover the top loosely with foil. Pull apart the pieces and fill your rolls or wraps. A Salsa (see p.112) will cool you down a bit.

CHERMOULA CHICKEN SKEWERS

This Moroccan *chermoula* marinade gives lots of flavour to both fish and chicken. *Chermoula* is sometimes used as a dip too. However, this one contains turmeric, which should be cooked before eating. If you ever want to use it as a dip, substitute a good pinch of saffron for the turmeric. Note that the chicken needs to marinate for at least 6 hours, but preferably overnight.

MAKES 12

500g skinless, boneless chicken breast
½ medium onion
2 garlic cloves
medium handful of flat-leaf parsley
1 tsp sweet paprika
1 tsp chilli flakes, or to taste
½ tsp ground cumin
½ tsp ground turmeric
zest and juice of ½ small (organic) lemon
1 tsp salt, or to taste
3 tbsp olive oil

Cut the chicken into fairly even-sized chunks (about 2cm) and put in a bowl. Put the remaining ingredients in a blender or food processor and blitz to make a paste. Mix well with the chicken and put in a glass or ceramic dish with a well-fitting cover. (Turmeric stains, so use plastic at your peril.) Chill for at least 6 hours or overnight.

You can cook the skewers in a stovetop grill pan or on the barbecue. If using a barbecue and bamboo skewers, soak the skewers for a few hours to delay charring.

Thread the pieces of chicken onto 12 skewers. Place them in a hot stovetop grill pan or on the barbecue and cook until compeletely cooked through, turning as needed. Serve in a tortilla, Seasoned Roti Wrapper or Pocket Bread (pp.15, 16), with Salsa Fresca, Mango Salsa or Mango Chutney (pp.112, 118, 120). Our favourite combination is with Seasoned Roti Wrappers and Mango Salsa.

LAMB SHAWARMA

▲▲▲▲▲▲▲▲▲▲▲▲▲▲▲▲▲▲▲▲

The type that is sliced from anonymous pressed meat that endlessly rotates on a vertical spit is well known all over the world – and holds mixed memories for many people. In the Middle East, better kinds of shawarma are made from succulent slow-roasted joints of lamb, but for a quick version at home you can even use a small piece of meat, as in this recipe. Note that the lamb needs to marinate overnight.

SERVES 4 (FILLING IS EASILY DOUBLED)

300g piece of tender lamb
   (e.g. from the leg)
1 tbsp lemon juice
2 tbsp olive oil
1–2 garlic cloves, crushed
¾ tsp ground cumin
½ tsp ground coriander
½ tsp ground cinnamon
¼ tsp ground ginger
⅛ tsp turmeric
⅛ tsp ground cardamom
⅛ tsp ground allspice
⅛ tsp ground black pepper
⅛ tsp chilli powder
salt, to taste

Slice the lamb thinly and put in a roomy bowl. Mix in the marinade ingredients with your hands, separating the slices as you go. Put it in a dish with a well-fitting cover (or use a large zipper freezer bag) and chill overnight. Next day, allow to come to room temperature.

Heat a large non-stick or well-seasoned frying pan or stovetop grill pan and lay some of the meat flat on it. Cook in batches, on both sides until pink on the inside or cooked through, so that you don't get a lot of moisture collecting at the base of the pan.

Sprinkle with salt to taste and serve immediately with 4 thick Flour Tortillas, Seasoned Roti Wrappers or 2 Pocket Breads (see pp.10, 15, 16) and your choice of the following groups: (a) tahini, thinly sliced tomato, red onion and cucumber; **or** (b) Salsa Fresca and Yogurt & Garlic Sauce with mint (see p.112 and p.126); **or** (c) Onion Relish and Yogurt & Cucumber Relish (see p.117 and p.121).

CHICKEN SHAWARMA

This is a slight variation on the Lamb Shawarma (see p.56) with a delicious collection of typical condiments. The homemade Garlic Sauce (see p.126) tastes a lot milder than you might expect and the salty pickled gherkins or cucumbers add both crunch and flavour. You will find the salty pickles in Middle Eastern or Mediterranean shops. Sweet or semi-sweet pickles will give a different flavour. By the way, don't be tempted to cut the chicken into small pieces and then stir-fry them to save time. They will turn into a curry: tasty, but wet with sauce. Trust me, I know. I learned the hard way. Marinate the chicken overnight for the best result.

MAKES 4

2 skinless, boneless chicken breasts (400g)
1 tbsp white wine vinegar
2 tbsp olive oil
2 garlic cloves, crushed
1 tsp ground cumin
¾ tsp ground coriander
½ tsp ground allspice
¼ tsp ground cinnamon
¼ tsp ground ginger
¼ tsp ground turmeric
¼ tsp ground cardamom
¼ tsp ground black pepper
¼ tsp chilli powder
scant ½ tsp salt, or to taste
4 Flour Tortillas (see p.10)

Remove the tenderloins, if present, then slice each chicken breast horizontally into 2 fairly even pieces. Rub in the marinade ingredients thoroughly into all of the chicken. Put it in a dish with a well-fitting cover (or use a large zipper freezer bag) and chill overnight.

Next day, allow to come to room temperature, then cook the chicken pieces until completely cooked through in a stovetop grill pan, on the barbecue, or under a preheated hot grill. Rest for a minute or two, then slice.

To serve, smear a spoonful of tahini along the centre of a warm tortilla. Top with a quarter of the sliced chicken. Drizzle a spoonful of Smooth Garlic Sauce (see p.126) over it and top with a handful of rocket and a few salted pickled gherkins or cucumber, cut into sticks. Tuck in the bottom, fold over and enjoy while still warm.

KEBAB WRAPS

A kebab can be made from many things, ranging from cheap (and often suspect) meat sliced from an interminably rotating block, to skewered chunks, or well-seasoned mince or roasted meat, tucked into a flatbread. The most magnificent version I've ever eaten was a meal shared in Konya with my Turkish friends Nevin and Nermin. The lamb had been slowly roasted overnight in a wood-fired oven and was so succulent you could have eaten it with a spoon. On ordering, we were given the choice of lean or fatty, and my companions laughed at my Western preoccupation with lean meat. It was sold by weight, so the portion was up to the diner. The required amount was deposited onto a flatbread and we were given a crisp green salad and yogurt sauce to accompany it. Absolute heaven. Here's a version with mince that is easy to make at home, with Turkish and Iraqi-Israeli serving suggestions.

MAKES 4

400g lean minced beef or lamb
2 garlic cloves, crushed
½ tsp salt, or to taste
1½ tsp ground cumin
1 tsp dried thyme
1 tsp dried oregano
1 tsp chilli flakes
1 tbsp dried breadcrumbs
1 egg, well beaten
about 2 tsp neutral-tasting oil, for cooking

You can make the kebabs and relish while the tortilla dough is resting. For the kebabs, knead everything (except the oil for cooking) together thoroughly and divide into 4 portions. Shape each one into a neat sausage about 22cm inches long, then flatten the sausage slightly to make a bar about 3cm wide. Wrap in clingfilm and chill until needed.

Prepare the tortillas. While the cooked tortillas are softening, cook the kebabs. Heat the oil in a non-stick pan and cook on both sides until cooked through. Alternatively, use a preheated hot grill if you prefer.

Put a kebab in the centre of a Flour Tortilla or *Dosti Roti* (see pp.10, 18) and top it Turkish style with some lettuce and a portion of Yogurt & Cucumber Relish (see p.121) and fold over to make a chunky roll. Or do it the Iraqi-Israeli way and spread hummus on the tortilla or *roti*, add a drizzle of tahini and the meat and top with Mango Chutney (see p.120) and a little finely shredded lettuce or cabbage. Serve immediately.

LAMB SOUVLAKI

Cheaper meats such as pork and chicken are often used in *souvlaki* in Greece nowadays, while lamb remains the ultimate treat. Although the marinade is designed to tenderise the meat, do start off with a good cut, such as a piece from the leg. Note that the meat needs to marinate overnight. If using bamboo skewers on a barbecue, soak them in water for a few hours to delay charring.

MAKES 4–5 SKEWERS (EASILY DOUBLED)

300g lamb (preferably from the leg)
1 tbsp red wine vinegar
1 tbsp lemon juice
2 tbsp olive oil
1–2 garlic cloves, crushed
1 tsp dried oregano
½ tsp dried thyme
¼ tsp freshly ground black pepper
4 thick Flour Tortillas or Seasoned Roti
    Wrappers (see p.10 and p.16)
sea salt

Cut the lamb into 2.5cm cubes and put in a non-reactive bowl with a well-fitting cover. Add the rest of the ingredients (the salt goes on after cooking) and mix to coat the meat well with the marinade. Cover and chill overnight. Next day, allow to come to room temperature.

Make the accompaniments. Prepare the tortillas or *rotis* and keep them warm.

Thread the meat onto skewers, leaving a small space between the chunks. Heat a stovetop grill pan until it is very hot and cook the meat to your liking. Alternatively, cook on the barbecue.

To serve, place a thick tortilla or *roti* on a plate and lay a skewer of meat on it. Sprinkle with sea salt to taste. Remove the skewer and top with your choice of accompaniments, such as Yogurt & Garlic Sauce with dill (see p.126), thinly sliced tomato and red onion, or roasted peppers. Fold over and tuck in the bottom so that nothing drips.

CHAPTER 3
PASTRIES & STUFFED SNACKS

JAMAICAN BEEF PATTIES

There's no escaping them in Jamaica. Roadside stands and even restaurants sell them. Fillings vary from chicken to prawns and vegetarian options, but beef is a firm favourite. And just as their ancestor, the meat pie or pasty, migrated from the British Isles to the Caribbean centuries ago, so have these accompanied Jamaican immigrants to Europe and North America. In Toronto, you will even find them slit and stuffed with shredded lettuce and sliced tomato.

MAKES 4

PASTRY

300g plain flour, plus extra for dusting

¼ tsp turmeric

generous ¼ tsp salt

50g vegetable shortening

75g butter, chilled and cubed,
    plus extra for greasing

90ml cold water, as needed

FILLING

1 tbsp groundnut or sunflower oil

1 medium onion, finely chopped

250g lean minced beef

1 large potato, peeled, cut into tiny cubes

2 tsp hot Madras curry powder

½ tsp salt, or to taste

2 tsp dried thyme

⅓ tsp ground allspice

a piece of (Scotch bonnet) chilli, to taste,
    finely chopped (optional)

beaten egg, for glazing

Put the flour, turmeric and salt in a large bowl. Add the shortening and butter, and rub between your fingertips until it looks like coarse breadcrumbs. It can be made in a food processor up to this stage. Pulse until well blended then transfer to a bowl. Add the water and bring it all together with your fingers to form a large ball. Wrap and chill.

For the filling, heat the oil in a heavy-based frying pan. Add the onion and cook until softened. Add the beef and break it up before adding the remaining ingredients. Cook until the potato is tender. Remove from the heat and taste for seasoning. Cool and use immediately or chill until needed.

Bring the pastry to room temperature. It will have tiny white flecks, but don't try to knead them in. Preheat oven to 180°C/Gas Mark 4 and grease a baking sheet. Divide the pastry into 4 portions and roll out on a lightly floured work surface to 20cm circles. Place a quarter of the filling on each, moisten the edge with water and fold over into a semi-circle. Crimp and seal the edges. Brush well with egg and prick several holes with a fork. Bake for 30–35 minutes until the tops are light golden and the pastry crisp. Eat warm from the oven or at room temperature.

INDONESIAN PASTIES
< PASTEL GORENG >

Just as colonial ties have led to Indian food becoming mainstream in Britain, Indonesian food has been absorbed into Dutch food culture. People cook it at home, eat it in restaurants or get it from takeaways, caterers and family-style groceries. These fried pasties are always available at takeaways and grocery counters for those in search of a satisfying snack. They take a little time to prepare, but are quite straightforward and rewarding to make at home.

MAKES 12

35g glass vermicelli noodles

1 skinless, boneless chicken breast
   (about 200g), finely chopped

1–2 garlic cloves, crushed

about ⅓ tsp salt, or to taste

2 tsp ground coriander

1 tsp ground cumin

1 tsp turmeric (optional)

1 tsp chilli flakes

75g carrot, finely chopped

75g green beans, finely chopped

2 tbsp groundnut or corn oil,
   plus extra for deep-frying

about 2 tbsp water

2 hard-boiled eggs, chopped

1 recipe Pastry for Frying (see p.22)

plain flour, for dusting

Make the filling first. Soak the noodles in boiling water for 15 minutes. Combine the chicken with the garlic, salt and spices. Heat the 2 tbsp oil in a frying pan or wok, add the chicken, carrot and beans and stir-fry briefly, then add about 2 tbsp water and cook until the vegetables are just tender. The liquid will evaporate, but if this happens too fast, add a little more to prevent the mixture from burning. Transfer to a bowl and stir in the chopped eggs. Drain the noodles well, snip them into short lengths with scissors and add to the filling. Taste and add salt if needed. Cool before using.

Divide the pastry into 12 portions. Roll each out very thinly to a 15cm disc on a lightly floured work surface. Spoon a portion of filling slightly off-centre onto a pastry disc and moisten the rim. Fold the pastry over to form a semi-circle, and trim and crimp with a fork. Alternatively, if you have a plastic pasty shaper, use that instead.

When all the pasties have been shaped, heat enough oil for deep-frying in a suitable pan to 180–185°C/350–365°F, or until a cube of bread browns in 30 seconds. Deep-fry in batches until light golden brown and crisp on both sides. Remove and drain on kitchen paper. Serve warm or at room temperature. Keep uneaten pasties refrigerated. Eat on their own or with Mango Chutney (see p.118) or Tamarind Sauce (see p.128).

CRISP & SPICY PACKETS
< MARTABAK >

▲▲▲▲▲▲▲▲▲▲▲▲▲▲▲▲▲▲▲▲

Known as *mutabbaq* in the Arabian Gulf and *murtabak* in Malaysia, *martabak* is Indonesian street food. It is usually prepared on the spot by street vendors who stretch the elastic dough to paper-thinness before folding it around the filling. This requires inordinate skill so, as a short-cut, use ready-made spring roll wrappers – shown to me by my friend Sri Owen, who knows all there is to know about Indonesian food.

MAKES 8 (ABOUT 9 X 9CM)

1 tsp ground coriander
¾ tsp ground cumin
¼–½ tsp ground ginger
½ tsp turmeric
¼ tsp ground allspice
¼–½ tsp chilli powder
about ¾ tsp salt (or to taste)
1 tbsp corn or groundnut oil,
    plus extra for cooking
1 large garlic clove, crushed
300g lean minced beef or lamb
3 spring onions, thinly sliced
small handful of coriander or flat-leaf
    parsley leaves, finely chopped
2 eggs, beaten (reserve 1 generous tbsp)
8 spring roll wrappers, about 20 x 20cm

Combine the spices with the salt in a small bowl and set aside. Heat 1 tbsp of oil in a non-stick pan, add the garlic and stir briefly until it starts to give off its aroma. Stir in the spice mixture, followed by the meat and stir-fry until the meat is cooked through. Transfer to a large bowl to cool right down. You can also chill it until needed, if necessary. Stir in the spring onions, coriander or parsley, and eggs when ready to cook.

Peel a wrapper off the stack and position it in a diamond shape. Stir the filling and put one-eighth of it in the centre of a wrapper. Spread it out to form a rough 8cm square, in the centre of the diamond. Brush some of the reserved egg around the 4 sides and fold 1 point over the filling. Bring the opposing point to just overlap this one. Next, fold the 2 remaining points inwards so that you get a square envelope-shaped packet. Press the top to seal. Set aside covered with clingfilm while you make the rest.

Heat a few tbsp of oil in a frying pan. Add as many packets as will comfortably fit and cook briefly until browned and crisp. Transfer to a serving plate lined with kitchen paper. Keep warm while you cook the rest. Serve them warm, whole or cut into two triangles. They are tasty on their own, but a little Tamarind Sauce (see p.128) adds an extra dimension.

SPRING ROLLS

▲▲▲▲▲▲▲▲▲▲▲▲▲▲▲▲▲▲▲▲▲▲▲▲

This perennial Asian favourite is made in varying shapes and sizes. Indonesians like a large chunky-looking roll, slit along the side to make room for a sauce. The Chinese prefer a slimmer article, while the Vietnamese go for a small, skinny and elegant one. Filipinos make all of these, adding 'lumpia' to the list (see p.26). Here in Holland, Vietnamese-style prevails.

MAKES 16 CIGAR-SHAPED ROLLS (15CM LONG)

25g rice vermicelli noodles

2 tbsp groundnut or sunflower oil, plus extra for deep-frying

small thumb-sized piece of fresh ginger, peeled and finely chopped

1 large garlic clove, crushed

100g chicken breast, cut into thin strips

75g carrot, cut into matchsticks

50g mangetout, cut into matchsticks

50g shiitake mushrooms, thinly sliced

75g bean sprouts

3 spring onions, thinly sliced

2 tbsp soy sauce

salt and freshly ground black pepper or chilli powder to taste

16 spring roll wrappers, about 20 x 20cm

1 egg white, loosely whisked

Soak the noodles in boiling water for 15 minutes. Drain thoroughly and snip into smaller lengths.

Meanwhile, heat 2 tbsp oil and stir-fry the ginger and garlic for a minute or two. Add the chicken and stir-fry for 2–3 minutes until almost seared. Throw in the carrot, mangetout and shiitake, and keep stir-frying for 2 or 3 minutes. The carrot and mangetout should be crunchy. Toss in the bean sprouts and spring onions, followed by the noodles, soy sauce, salt and pepper or chilli powder, and stir-fry for a minute more to mix the flavours. Cool completely, in a colander so that excess moisture drains out.

Lay a wrapper in a diamond shape on the work surface. Brush the edges with egg white. Put a small portion of filling slightly below the middle. Shape the filling into a horizontal line about 15cm long. Fold the bottom point of the wrapper over the filling, then fold the sides inwards. Roll up neatly. Brush the point with more egg white before pressing it to seal. Shape the others.

Heat oil for deep-frying in a suitable pan to about 185–190°C/365–375°, or until a cube of bread browns in 30 seconds. Deep-fry the rolls in batches, until crisp and light golden brown. Remove and drain on kitchen paper. Serve hot with Nuoc Cham (p.129), Mango Chutney (p.118) or sweet chilli sauce.

VEGETABLE SAMOSAS

This version of the classic Indian snack is by far the best known. The pastry here is the 'authentic' one, but takes practice as it is prone to tearing. Pastry for Frying is easier to handle, if less crisp.

MAKES 12

PASTRY (or ½ recipe Pastry for Frying, p.22)
125g plain flour, plus extra for dusting
¼ tsp salt
1 tbsp groundnut or sunflower oil
about 65ml very hot water, or as needed

FILLING
300g waxy potatoes, cut into small dice
75g green peas, thawed if frozen
½ tsp coriander seeds
½ tsp cumin seeds
½ tsp fennel seeds
½ tsp black mustard seeds
½ tsp nigella seeds
¼–½ tsp chilli flakes
generous ¼ tsp salt, or to taste
2 tbsp neutral-tasting oil,
   plus extra for oiling and frying
2-in piece of fresh ginger, finely chopped

Combine all the pastry ingredients to make a firm dough. Shape into a ball, cover and rest at room temperature for ½–2 hours.

Cook the potatoes until just tender and drain. Add the peas and set aside.

Put the coriander, cumin, fennel and black mustard seeds in a small dry frying pan and toast, shaking the pan. Remove from the heat when the mustard seeds start popping. Cool, then crush with a mortar and pestle. Add the nigella, chilli and salt and set aside.

Heat 2 tbsp of oil in a non-stick frying pan, add ginger and stir-fry for 1–2 minutes. Add potato mix and stir-fry for a few minutes. Add spices and stir-fry for 1 minute. Cool.

Divide the pastry into 6 portions. Roll each out on a silicone mat to a circle 15cm in diameter. Dust only if absolutely necessary. Cut each circle in half and moisten the rims lightly with water. Put a dessertspoonful of filling on one half of each semi-circle and fold over along the straight side, pressing to seal this side, to make a quarter circle. Pick up and hold like a cone. Add more filling if needed. Pinch the top edge together about halfway, then pinch the rest of the pastry at right angles to this, to make a small pyramid. Place on an oiled plate.

Heat enough oil for deep-frying in a suitable pan to 190°C/375°F, or until a cube of bread browns in 30 seconds. Fry in batches until crisp and golden. Drain on kitchen paper. Serve hot with Mango Chutney (p.118).

BAKES & SALTFISH

▲▲▲▲▲▲▲▲▲▲▲▲▲▲▲▲▲▲▲▲▲▲▲▲▲

Made at home or sold by street vendors, this combination is a Caribbean cult favourite. A 'bake' is actually a chewy fried bread with a cavity that is filled with a tasty fish mixture. My sister is the bake-and-saltfish expert in our family, so I turned to her for advice. Overhearing us, our father hastened to add his bit: 'Black pepper, don't forget the black pepper. Plenty of it.' And there you have it: Guyanese love their black pepper in bakes and it contrasts well with the slight sweetness. If you don't feel up to the chewy pepperiness of the real thing, use the *Lángos* recipe (p.21) instead, making 8 smaller breads and folding them over the saltfish.

MAKES 8

BAKES
350g plain flour, plus extra for dusting
2¼ tsp baking powder
scant ¼ tsp salt
2 tbsp granulated sugar
¼ tsp finely ground black pepper
¼ tsp ground cinnamon (optional)
about 240ml tepid water, or as needed
neutral-tasting oil, for deep-frying

SALTFISH FILLING
2–3 tbsp olive oil
1 large white onion, finely chopped
2 large garlic cloves, crushed
350g desalted saltfish (see p.154), flaked
2 medium tomatoes, deseeded
    and chopped
1–2 red chillies, thinly sliced
juice of ½ lime, or to taste
1 scant tbsp thyme leaves
    or 2 tbsp chopped flat-leaf parsley

For the bakes, knead the ingredients together to make a supple, fairly soft dough. Shape the still rough dough into a ball, put it in a bowl and cover with clingfilm. Rest at room temperature for about 30 minutes. The sugar will melt during this period and the dough will be softer.

Heat enough oil for deep-frying in a suitable pan to about 180°C/350°F, or until a cube of bread browns in 30 seconds. Re-knead the dough briefly and divide into 8 balls. Roll out to a neat 9–10cm disc, dusting as needed. Deep-fry in batches in the hot oil. They will rise to the surface and puff up. Cook to light golden on both sides. Overcooking will make them even chewier. Remove and drain on kitchen paper.

For the filling, heat the olive oil in a frying pan, add the onion and garlic, and cook briefly. Add the saltfish, tomatoes, chillies and thyme, if using, and heat through. Don't allow it to become pulpy. Stir in the lime juice (and parsley if using) and stuff into the warm split bakes.

STEAMED FILLED BUNS

▲▲▲▲▲▲▲▲▲▲▲▲▲▲▲▲▲▲▲▲▲▲

Steamed buns have been known in China for more than 2000 years, first in the wheat-eating North and later spreading to the rest of the country and far beyond. Use pork if you prefer, and adapt the seasoning to suit your taste. This satisfying snack is equally good eaten warm or at room temperature, on its own or with a soy-based dipping sauce. You'll need a steamer.

MAKES 8

DOUGH
300g plain flour
2 tsp granulated sugar
2 tsp easy-blend dried yeast
1 tbsp neutral-tasting oil
about 170ml warm water

FILLING
1 spring onion, coarsely chopped
2.5cm piece of fresh ginger, peeled and
   thinly sliced
2 garlic cloves, crushed
300g boneless chicken (or pork), chopped
1 tbsp soy sauce
2 tsp sesame oil
1 tsp rice or cider vinegar
½ tsp granulated sugar
40g water chestnuts, chopped
¼–½ tsp salt, to taste

Combine the ingredients to make a soft dough. Knead into a ball, put in a bowl, cover with clingfilm and leave in a warm, draught-free place until doubled in size.

Prepare the filling while the dough is rising. Put the spring onion, ginger and garlic

into a food processor and pulse until fine. Add the remaining ingredients, except for the water chestnuts, and blitz until finely ground. Mix in the water chestnuts and chill. Remove from the fridge 30 minutes before needed and divide into 8 portions.

Knock back the risen dough and knead again very briefly. Divide it into 8 balls. Take 1 ball and flatten to a 10–12cm disc. Moisten the rim with water. Put a portion of filling in the centre and pleat the dough around this, pinching to seal. Place it on a small square of greaseproof paper in the steamer basket. Seal-side up will give a more rugged effect, which some people like, but I usually put them seal-side down. Shape the rest. Leave for about 30 minutes in a warm, draught-free place. They should be puffed up but not yet quite doubled in size. If you don't have enough steamer capacity to steam all at the same time, leave some in a slightly cooler place to delay the rising process.

Steam for about 15 minutes until the dough has set and the filling is cooked through.

POTSTICKERS

If you've never come across these Chinese dumplings before, it's high time you tried them. They are not the traditional steamed or boiled kind. Instead, they are fried and lightly steamed in the same pan, creating a lovely bottom crust. You can buy frozen *gyoza* or dumpling skins in Asian shops. Wonton skins are too thin for this method and spring roll wrappers create a different texture, but can be used at a pinch. They freeze well. Thaw in the fridge and reheat in a non-stick pan lightly coated with oil, over a low heat, until crisped up.

MAKES 24

24 *gyoza*/dumpling skins (10cm), thawed
about 4 tbsp groundnut or corn oil, for frying
about 3 tbsp water, or as needed
dipping sauce of your choice, to serve

FILLING
200g Chinese leaves
1 tsp salt
300g pork or chicken, minced
1–2 garlic cloves, grated
about 2.5cm piece of fresh ginger, peeled
    and grated
2 spring onions, finely chopped
2–3 tsp soy sauce
2 tsp sesame oil
1 tsp rice vinegar

Select a large, non-stick, heavy-based frying pan and a lid that will fit.

Shred the Chinese leaves as thinly as you can, then chop them into shorter lengths. Put in a colander and mix in the salt. Leave to drain for about 30–40 minutes. Squeeze as much water as you can from the wilted leaves. Mix thoroughly with the remaining filling ingredients and chill for 15–20 minutes.

Place 1 tbsp of filling in the centre of a dumpling skin. Moisten the rim with water. Fold 2 opposing corners inwards to meet and cover the filling. Pinch and press the edges to seal. Shape all the dumplings the same way.

Heat half of the oil in the pan (or all, if the pan will hold all the dumplings comfortably). Arrange them quickly, seam-side up, and allow the bases to brown. Add about 3 tbsp water and cover immediately as it will spit and hiss. Cook for a few minutes until the skins no longer look raw. Remove the lid and turn the dumplings over. Allow them to brown on the base once the water has evaporated until crisp. Cook any remaining dumplings in the same way.

Serve hot with plain soy sauce, a mixture of soy sauce and vinegar, or *Nuoc Cham* (see p.129).

MIDDLE EASTERN MEAT 'PIZZAS' & TURNOVERS
< LAHMACUN & SFIHA >

▲▲▲▲▲▲▲▲▲▲▲▲▲▲▲▲▲▲▲▲▲▲▲▲

Known as *lahmacun* in Turkey and *lahm bil'ajeen* in many Arabic-speaking countries, these are best described as meat pizzas: a thin round or oval crust with a topping of meat and/or seasonal vegetables covering the entire surface. They can be folded into turnovers too. In Brazil, for instance, the popular street snack *(e)sfiha* has its roots in the Arab *sfiha*, which is made by enclosing the filling in the dough to form a triangular turnover.

> ### MAKES 4 'PIZZAS' (20CM)
> ### OR 8 TRIANGULAR TURNOVERS

1 recipe Basic Yeast Dough (see p.11)
plain flour, for dusting

TOPPING
300g lean minced lamb or beef
1 red pepper, very finely chopped
½ tsp salt, or to taste
handful of flat-leaf parsley, finely chopped
2 garlic cloves, crushed
½ tsp chilli flakes, or to taste
1 ½ tbsp tomato purée

Make the dough as directed on p.11. Cut 4 rectangles of baking parchment, about 24cm square. Preheat the oven (and pizza stone) to 225°C/Gas Mark 7.

Combine topping ingredients in a bowl and cover. Set aside at cool room temperature.

Knock back the risen dough and knead briefly. Divide it into 4 balls. Roll out 1 ball on a lightly floured work surface to a circle about 22cm in diameter and put it on a piece of baking parchment. If it shrinks on the paper, flatten it out again. Spread a quarter of the filling on the dough, up to the edges. Place on a baking sheet if using. Make the rest in the same way.

(If baking on a pizza stone, use a rimless metal sheet to slide the pizzas into the oven, on the paper.) Bake the pizzas for about 4 minutes, then slip off the paper and bake for another 4–8 minutes, or until cooked through and golden brown around the edges. The shorter time is for the pizza stone.

Turnovers: Use 1 finely chopped onion instead of pepper. Divide the dough into 8. Roll out thinly to 20cm circles. Put a portion of filling in the centres. Fold the dough over to enclose almost completely and shape roughly into large triangles with 14cm sides. Bake on a baking sheet for 13–15 minutes. These will be softer than the flat pizzas.

GALICIAN TUNA PIE
< EMPANADA GALLEGA CON ATÚN >

▲▲▲▲▲▲▲▲▲▲▲▲▲▲▲▲▲▲▲▲▲▲▲▲

Empanadas are more usually small fried pastries, but this tasty variation from northwestern Spain is baked as a large pie. In former days, when few households owned a domestic oven, housewives would make pies with fillings concocted from seasonal surplus – fish, vegetables etc. – and take them to be baked by the local baker. The individual decorations each put on her pie ensured that every pie returned to the right home. Nowadays it is widely sold in eateries and supermarkets, whole or portioned, and tuna is one of the most popular fillings.

**MAKES 1 LARGE PIE
(SERVES 4 AS A SNACK)**

FILLING
60ml olive oil
1 large onion, finely chopped
2 tsp (sweet) paprika
200g canned chopped tomatoes
2 x 160g cans tuna in olive oil,
    drained and flaked
1 tbsp small capers or chopped olives
    (optional)

CASING
250g plain flour, plus extra for dusting
1½ tsp easy-blend dried yeast
½ tsp salt
1 tsp granulated sugar
50ml liquid from the onion and
    tomato mixture
about 125ml warm water (body
    temperature)
beaten egg, for glazing

Heat the oil in a frying pan and add the onion. Yes, it is a generous amount of oil, but most of it will go into the dough shortly. Fry over a medium heat for a few minutes until softened. Add the paprika and give it a good stir. Then add the tomatoes and simmer for about 5 minutes. Remove from the heat and tip the contents of the frying pan into a heatproof colander placed over a bowl. Drain for a few minutes. Remove the colander and place over a plate. Measure out 3 tbsp of the liquid collected in the bowl and use this for the yeast dough. In the unlikely event of not having enough liquid, make up the shortfall with olive oil. Add the tuna and capers or olives, if using, to the cooled mixture.

[method continues overleaf]

GALICIAN TUNA PIE, cont.

Combine the ingredients for the dough and knead well for several minutes. The dough should be soft but not sticky, and the cooking liquid will give it a lovely colour as well as flavour. Shape the dough into a ball and put it in a bowl. Cover with clingfilm or a damp tea towel and leave in a warm, draught-free place until doubled in size.

Knock back the dough and knead it briefly until smooth.

Preheat the oven to 200°C/Gas Mark 6.

Roll the dough out very thinly on a silicone mat or other surface dusted with flour. Aim for a rectangle about 40 x 30cm. Trim the edges to make them straight. Cut the dough in half and use the rolling pin to transfer one half to the sheet. If it shrinks, press it back out to its original size. It should be very thin. Top evenly with the filling, leaving about 1.5cm free on all sides. Moisten this rim with water. Top with the second piece of dough and stretch it if necessary to cover the filling and come down to the edge of the first piece. Press to seal. Now take your index or middle finger and push then press the dough inwards to create a scalloped pattern. Prick a few holes in the top with a fork and press the top with both hands to remove as much air as possible. Roll out the trimmings extremely thinly and use to make some decorations for the top, such as stripes, fishes, flowers. Brush well with beaten egg and prick again in several places with a fork.

Bake immediately in the oven until nicely browned, about 30–35 minutes. Cool on a wire rack. Eat at room temperature, but keep leftovers refrigerated.

STUFFED POTATO CAKES

▲▲▲▲▲▲▲▲▲▲▲▲▲▲▲▲▲▲▲▲▲▲▲

Delicious potato cakes are made all over the world and seasoning varies according to regional preferences. These are in the style of Indian *Alu Chaap* (potato chops), and their Middle Eastern cousins *Batata Charp* or *Batata Chap*.

MAKES 8 (ABOUT 9CM)

500g floury potatoes (peeled weight), peeled and cut into even-sized chunks
salt, as needed
1 egg, well beaten
1 tbsp plain flour, or as needed, plus extra for dusting
3–4 tbsp neutral-tasting oil, for cooking

FILLING
Spice mixture: ¾ tsp each fennel, cumin, coriander and black mustard seeds, ¼ tsp chilli powder, ½ tsp turmeric, ¼ tsp ground cinnamon
1 tbsp corn or groundnut oil
1 small onion
1 large garlic clove, crushed
250g lean minced lamb or beef
⅓ tsp salt, or to taste

Boil the potatoes in a pan of salted water until tender. Drain and cool.

For the filling, toast the whole spices in a dry pan, shaking it frequently. Remove from the heat as soon as the mustard seeds start to pop. Cool and crush with a mortar and pestle. Add the other spices.

Heat the oil in a non-stick pan, add the onion and garlic, and cook for a few minutes until soft. Add the mince, stirring to break it up. Add the spice mixture and salt to taste and allow the mince to cook through. Set aside to cool.

Put about 4 tbsp flour on a plate and line a tray with clingfilm. Mash the cooled potatoes thoroughly. Add salt if needed. Work the egg and the 1 tbsp flour into the potato with a fork to make a smooth mixture, then divide into 8 pieces. Roll a piece in the flour on the plate, then flatten to a 10cm disc. Top with one-eighth of the filling and coax the potato around the filling to enclose. Dip both sides in the flour and flatten to a 9cm cake. Place on the lined tray and make the others.

Heat 1 generous tbsp of oil in a non-stick frying pan and cook the cakes in batches over a medium-low heat until both sides are golden brown, about 4–5 minutes each side. The sides will remain pale. Serve immediately, with Quick Coconut Chutney (p.122) or Mango Chutney (p.118).

CHAPTER 4
SAVOURY CAKES & FRITTERS

ASIAN FISH CAKES

Cakes of this kind, sold by street vendors or prepared at home in Asia, make delicious appetisers, but can also be served in wraps.

MAKES 16

450g firm white fish fillets, e.g. cod*
1 lemongrass stalk, trimmed and sliced
1 bird's-eye chilli, deseeded if wished
tiny handful of coriander leaves
2 spring onions, roughly chopped
2 tsp cornflour
½ tsp salt, or to taste
generous ¼ tsp turmeric
1 egg white
groundnut or corn oil,
    for oiling and cooking

*If using frozen fish, thaw about 550–600g, as there will be weight loss in water as it thaws. Weigh the thawed fish before using it.

Pat the fish dry and cut into coarse chunks.

Put the lemongrass, chilli, coriander, spring onions, cornflour, salt and turmeric in a food processor and pulse until fine. Add the fish and egg white, and pulse until paste-like. Chill for 30–60 minutes. If you leave it much longer, water will start to seep out.

Remove the fish paste from the fridge and divide the mixture into 16 ping-pong ball-sized pieces, flattening them slightly into cakes. Arrange on an oiled plate.

Heat a few tbsp of oil in a large non-stick pan and fry the cakes for 2–3 minutes on each side, or until appetisingly flecked with brown and cooked through.

Serve hot with Tamarind Sauce (see p.128) or *Nuoc Cham* (see p.129) or put them in a wrap.

SALMON PATTIES WITH MUSHY PEAS

These patties have no potato, just the pure fish for maximum flavour. The accompanying mushy peas not only taste good, but they add a burst of colour. The recipe can go any way you like. Make tiny cakes and serve garnished with the mushy peas as an appetiser, make medium-sized oval patties and put them in a wrap of your choice, or make large round patties and tuck them into Butter Flaps (see p.12).

> **MAKES 16 TINY CAKES,**
> **12 MEDIUM OVAL PATTIES OR**
> **8 LARGE ROUND PATTIES**

400g skinless salmon fillet
small handful of dill, roughly chopped
1 tbsp cornflour
⅓ tsp salt, or to taste
2–3 tsp mild mustard,
   depending on the strength
freshly ground black pepper to taste
butter, or groundnut or corn oil,
   for oiling and cooking

MUSHY PEAS
300g fresh or frozen peas
1–2 tbsp butter or olive oil
salt and freshly ground pepper
few mint leaves, finely chopped

Cut the fish into small chunks. Put it in a food processor with the rest of the ingredients (except the fat) and give it a couple of whizzes. You want to keep some texture, so do this in short bursts. Chill for 30–60 minutes, or until firm enough to handle.

Meanwhile, boil the peas in unsalted water until just tender. Overcooking will spoil the colour as well as flavour. Drain, reserving a few tbsp of the liquid. Add the rest of the ingredients and use a stick (or regular) blender to make a purée. Add a little of the cooking water if you want it less thick. Adjust the seasoning as desired. Keep warm until ready to serve.

Remove the fish mixture from the fridge and shape into 16 small plum-shaped cakes, or 12 oval patties, or 8 round patties. Arrange on an oiled plate.

Heat a few tbsp of butter or oil in a large non-stick pan and fry the cakes on each side until appetisingly flecked with brown and just cooked through. Drain on kitchen paper and serve with the mushy peas.

FALAFEL

You no longer have to travel to the Middle East for your falafel fix, as it is sold in almost any city you care to name. It isn't that hard to make at home either. Professional falafel-makers use an ejector-scoop, a necessity due to the volume of their turnover. It is a lovely piece of equipment to have, but fear not: the mixture can be effectively shaped by hand too. Note that the chickpeas will need to soak overnight.

MAKES ABOUT 18

250g dried chickpeas
about 2 litres water
2 spring onions, chopped
2 garlic cloves, crushed
small handful of flat-leaf parsley
    or coriander
¾ tsp ground cumin
½ tsp ground coriander
¼–½ tsp chilli powder
¾ tsp salt, or to taste
½ tsp baking powder
2 tbsp plain flour
neutral-tasting oil, for deep-frying and oiling

Rinse the chickpeas and put them in a large bowl. Cover with water and soak overnight. Next day, drain the chickpeas and place in a food processor. Add the remaining ingredients, except the oil. Use short bursts to obtain a smooth (but not mushy) mixture. When you press a handful together, it should stay in place and not fall apart. Chill the mixture for 30 minutes–2 hours.

Heat enough oil for deep-frying in a suitable pan to about 175–180°C/347–350°F, or until a cube of bread browns in 30 seconds. Take walnut-sized portions of the mixture and compact them between your hands to make a ball, then flatten slightly to make a patty. These will cook faster and more evenly than balls. Put them on an oiled plate. When you are about halfway through shaping the mixture and the oil is hot enough, fry a batch until browned and cooked through. Drain on kitchen paper and keep warm.

Continue shaping and frying. You will need to fry in 2–3 batches, depending on the size of your pan.

Serve as a cocktail snack with tahini or the Yogurt & Garlic Sauce (p.126), or even Tamarind Sauce (p.128). Stuff into a Pocket Bread (p.15) or wrap in a Flour Tortilla (p.8) or *roti* and add the sauces, along with Salsa Fresca (see p.112) and shredded lettuce. If stuffing them into a wrap or bread, break up the falafel patties roughly so that you get crunchy and soft bits and the sauce can penetrate the patties.

CARIBBEAN FISH CAKES

▲▲▲▲▲▲▲▲▲▲▲▲▲▲▲▲▲▲▲▲▲▲

They come in many variations and go by numerous names, from simple generic 'fish cake' to the colourful Jamaican 'stamp-and-go', which conjures up images of impatient customers stamping their feet at a roadside stall, while they wait for their fritters to be fried so that they can go. In Barbados, a favourite sandwich is 'bread-and-two': a bread roll filled with two fish cakes. What they all have in common is that saltfish is used to give flavour and they are generally flour-based. Note that they are quite filling, so if you serve them as an appetiser, you probably won't need a lot of food to follow – unless you can restrict yourself to one or two. They go very well with summery drinks. Here's my version.

MAKES ABOUT 18

neutral-tasting oil, for deep-frying
150g plain flour
1 tsp baking powder
¼ tsp salt, or to taste
150g desalted saltfish (see p.154), flaked
2 spring onions, thinly sliced
1 red chilli, finely chopped
2 eggs, well beaten
about 75ml water

Heat enough oil for deep-frying in a suitable pan to 180–185°C/350–365°F, or until a cube of bread browns in 30 seconds.

Mix the flour, baking powder and salt together in a bowl. Add the other ingredients and mix to make a very thick batter.

Dip a dessertspoonful of the batter. Scrape it off into a second dessertspoon, then use the first spoon to slide it out into the hot oil. It sounds fiddly, but this way, you get neater balls than by just sliding it off the first spoon. Fry in batches until golden and cooked through. To check, split one open with 2 forks; the middle should not be raw. Remove and drain on kitchen paper.

Serve warm with lime wedges, Tamarind Sauce (p.128), Mango Chutney or Salsa (pp.118, 120) or bought West Indian hot sauce.

CRISP PRAWN FRITTERS
< UKOY >

▲▲▲▲▲▲▲▲▲▲▲▲▲▲▲▲▲▲▲▲▲▲▲▲▲▲▲▲▲

At a market in southern Spain, I saw a smiling chubby man in a motorised wheelchair surrounded by friends. He was playing a game involving a cup and a pile of grey pebbles. Intrigued, I approached. To my amazement, the pebbles appeared to be alive. They were! And they were tiny live shrimp, jumping about jerkily as they were scooped up and put into paper cones for the waiting customers. They were destined for the delicious crisp fritters known as *tortillitas de camarones*. I suppose that you, like me, will have no ready source of live tiny shrimp and that is what the dish is all about: whole unpeeled shrimp fried in a chickpea flour batter. But don't despair. Here's an equally delightful fritter from the other side of the world. Bought from a street stall, it is a popular afternoon snack or *merienda* in the Philippines, but has become very fashionable as an appetiser in fancy restaurants too.

MAKES 10–12

75g plain flour
35g cornflour
1 egg, well beaten
80ml water
2 tsp fish sauce
freshly ground black pepper
100g peeled and deveined prawns,
    chopped
60g bean sprouts
40g carrot, cut into thin matchsticks
1 spring onion, thinly sliced
groundnut or corn oil,
    for deep-frying and oiling

Sift the flour and cornflour in a bowl. Add the egg, water, fish sauce and black pepper to taste and whisk to make a smooth batter. Cover and rest for 10–15 minutes. Stir in the remaining ingredients, except the oil.

Heat enough oil for deep-frying in a suitable pan to about 180°C/350°F, or until a cube of bread browns in 30 seconds.

The fritters should be as flat as possible so take a wide metal spatula and oil it. (In the Philippines, they use banana or cacao leaves.) Dip a soup spoon (the kind you eat your soup with) of the mixture and deposit it on the spatula. Flatten it a little. Lower the spatula into the oil, then slide the *ukoy* off into the oil. If you can't manage that, just drop them into the oil straight from the spoon, but they will be chunkier and not as crisp. Fry on both sides until cooked through. Remove and drain on kitchen paper.

Serve immediately with a fruity vinegar, with optional chilli and garlic slices in it.

VEGETABLE FRITTERS IN CHICKPEA BATTER

▲▲▲▲▲▲▲▲▲▲▲▲▲▲▲▲▲▲▲▲▲▲▲▲▲

In Bengali-speaking areas, they call them *beguni*, but I grew up with the Hindi variation *baigani*. Both are derived from the word for aubergine, and these fritters are immensely popular in Indo-Caribbean households. The batter works well with other vegetables too. Onions and slender green beans are a favourite in my house, but use whatever firm vegetable takes your fancy, such as cauliflower or broccoli florets and small asparagus. In Guyana, we like to be able to taste the batter, so we make a thicker coating than many might like. If you find the batter too thick for you, add a little more water when preparing it. These delicious snacks should be eaten hot before they have time to go limp.

> FOR 1 MEDIUM AUBERGINE,
> 1 LARGE WHITE ONION AND
> A HANDFUL OF GREEN BEANS

100g chickpea flour (*besan*)
100g plain flour
1 tsp salt
1½ tsp ground cumin
½–1 tsp chilli flakes
250ml water (or more for a thinner batter)
1 medium aubergine
salt, for sprinkling
1 large white onion
handful of green beans
groundnut or corn oil, for deep-frying

Sift the flours into a bowl and combine with the other dry ingredients. Add the water and whisk to make a smooth batter. Cover with clingfilm and leave for about 15 minutes.

Meanwhile, slice the aubergine just over 5mm thick and place in a colander. Sprinkle lightly with salt and mix them up to get the salt on all the slices. When ready to use, pat away the beads of moisture with kitchen paper. (Only aubergines need to be salted in this way.) Leave the beans whole and cut the onion into 5mm slices.

Heat enough oil for deep-frying in a suitable pan to 180–185°C/350–365°F, or until a cube of bread browns in 30 seconds. Dip a slice of aubergine in the batter and shake to get rid of the excess. Put it in the hot oil and repeat with a few more slices. Don't overcrowd the pan. Fry on both sides until crisp and nicely browned. Remove and drain on kitchen paper. Cook the rest in the same way.

Serve hot: plain, with Spicy Mango Chutney (see p.118) or Tamarind Sauce (see p.128).

COURGETTE & FETA CAKES
< KABAKLI MÜCVER >

▲▲▲▲▲▲▲▲▲▲▲▲▲▲▲▲▲▲▲▲▲▲▲

These Turkish courgette cakes make a fine snack at any time of day, but also do well as an appetiser. You can wrap them in a tortilla or *roti*.

MAKES ABOUT 1 DOZEN

350g courgette
2 spring onions, thinly sliced
50g plain flour
¼ tsp salt
freshly ground black pepper
2 tbsp finely chopped dill
1 red chilli, finely chopped (optional)
100g feta cheese, crumbled
2 eggs, well beaten
3–4 tbsp olive oil, for cooking

Line a large bowl with a cheesecloth or loosely woven tea towel. Grate the courgette coarsely into the bowl. Twist the cloth to squeeze out as much moisture as you can, then transfer the courgette to the bowl. Add the spring onions, flour, salt, pepper, dill and chilli, if using, then add the feta and combine well with all the other ingredients. Mix in the eggs.

Heat 2 tbsp olive oil in a large non-stick frying pan. Spoon 6 or 7 heaps into the pan, about 2 slightly rounded tbsp per heap. Flatten the tops with the back of the spoon to a diameter of 6–7cm and cook for 4–5 minutes on each side. The cakes should be dark golden brown and cooked through. Drain on kitchen paper and keep warm if you plan to serve them that way.

Add a little more oil to the pan. Give the mixture a stir to mix in any liquid that has leached out and cook the second batch of cakes.

Serve warm or at room temperature with Yogurt & Garlic Sauce (see p.126) on the side.

SPICY SWEETCORN CAKES
< PERGEDEL JAGUNG >

▲▲▲▲▲▲▲▲▲▲▲▲▲▲▲▲▲▲▲▲▲▲▲▲▲▲▲

'Pergedel' denotes a fried savoury patty in Indonesia. It is the local transcription of the Dutch word *frikadel*, which was used until the mid-twentieth century in Holland to mean a minced meat patty and has now come to mean a low-quality fried sausage of indeterminate composition. Corn is a relative newcomer to the Indonesian food scene, supposedly only arriving in the sixteenth century with the Spaniards, but is now firmly ingrained in Indonesian cooking traditions.

**MAKES 8 CAKES
(7–8CM)**

275g fresh, frozen or well-drained canned
   sweetcorn kernels
1 spring onion, thinly sliced
1 garlic clove, crushed
¼ tsp chilli or cayenne powder
1 tsp ground coriander
generous ¼ tsp ground cumin
¼ tsp salt (more for fresh or frozen)
½ tsp baking powder
2 tbsp plain flour
1 egg, well beaten
3–4 tbsp corn or groundnut oil, for frying

If using fresh sweetcorn kernels, blanch them for a minute or so in boiling water. Purée half of the corn and put it in a bowl with the whole kernels. Add the remaining ingredients, except for the oil, and stir well to combine.

Heat 1½–2 tbsp of oil in a non-stick frying pan. Spoon heaped tbsp of the batter into the pan and flatten with the back of a spoon to a diameter of 7–8cm. Leave enough room in the pan for manoeuvring. Cook over a medium heat for about 3 minutes on each side. If any corn kernels escape, simply press them back into the moist sides. Remove and drain on kitchen paper, and keep warm if you plan to serve them that way.

Add a little more oil to the pan and cook the second batch.

Serve hot, warm or even at room temperature, optionally with a soy-based dipping sauce such as *Nuoc Cham* (see p.129) or even a chutney or salsa. They will be at their lightest eaten hot or warm.

CHAPTER 5
PANCAKES & GRIDDLE CAKES

SIZZLING CAKES
< BANH XEO >

The Vietnamese word 'xeo' (pronounced 'sayo') represents the sizzling sound made when the batter for these pancakes hits the pan. Ingredients, preparation and names vary across the country, and southerners are reputedly more generous with the filling than northerners. Eat them the Vietnamese way: wrap bits in lettuce leaves with herbs to taste, before dipping in *Nuoc Cham* (p.129). Or serve folded, as a wrap in its own right, doubling the amount of filling.

MAKES 4

BATTER
125g regular (non-glutinous) rice flour
generous ½ tsp turmeric
¼ tsp salt
175ml coconut milk
175ml water
1–2 spring onions, thinly sliced

FILLING
100g pork or chicken breast, thinly sliced
1–2 garlic cloves, crushed
1 tbsp soy sauce
neutral-tasting oil, for cooking
1 small onion, sliced lengthways
100g prawns, peeled, deveined, and
  chopped if large
75g bean sprouts
salt if needed
mint, (Thai) basil, coriander leaves, to serve

Sift the rice flour, turmeric and salt into a bowl. Add the coconut milk and water and whisk well to make thin, lump-free batter. Stir in the spring onions and leave for 30–60 minutes. Stir well before using and before ladling out each pancake.

Mix the meat with the garlic and 1½ tsp of the soy sauce. Cover and chill until needed. Cook the filling just before you make the pancakes. Heat 1 tbsp of oil in a wok and stir-fry the onion briefly. Add the meat and stir-fry until almost cooked. Stir in the prawns. When they are almost cooked through, add the bean sprouts and remaining soy sauce. Remove from the heat and keep warm.

Put 1 tsp of oil in a 23–24cm non-stick frying pan over a high heat. Keep the heat high. Add about 75ml of the batter and swirl quickly but gently to cover the base of the pan. (The batter is delicate.) Cook until crisp on the bottom and dry on top. Spoon a quarter of the filling over half of the pancake, fold over and slide onto a plate. Keep warm. Make the rest in the same way.

Give everyone an individual dipping bowl. Cut each pancake into 4–5 pieces. Take a flexible lettuce leaf and top with the pancake and some mint, (Thai) basil and/or coriander leaves to taste. Fold into a parcel, dip in *Nuoc Cham* (see p.129) and enjoy.

SEMOLINA DOSAS
< RAVA DOSA >

▲▲▲▲▲▲▲▲▲▲▲▲▲▲▲▲▲▲▲▲▲▲▲

The batter for this semolina version of the popular South Indian breakfast and snack does not need to ferment like the traditional rice and lentil one, and is ready to use after a mere half an hour. During the resting time, you can whip up a batch of Quick Coconut Chutney (p.122) to go with it. Mango Chutney (p.118) is also excellent. I find them tasty enough to eat as they are too, or with a few drops of lime juice. For something more substantial, use the dosas to scoop up or roll the filling for Vegetable Samosas (p.71); squeeze some lime juice over the cooked filling and sprinkle on some chopped coriander, if you like.

MAKES 6

100g fine semolina
50g regular (non-glutinous) rice flour
2 tbsp plain flour
scant ½ tsp salt, or to taste
½ tsp ground cumin
pinch of ground black pepper
450ml lukewarm water
1 green chilli, finely chopped
1 tbsp finely chopped coriander
40–50g butter or ghee, for cooking

Combine the flours, salt and spices in a bowl. Add the water and whisk to make a <u>very</u> thin batter. Feel with your fingers for lumps and rub to dissolve. Stir in the chilli and coriander, cover with clingfilm and leave for 30 minutes–1 hour.

When ready to cook the dosas, melt some butter or ghee in a 23cm non-stick frying pan. Give the batter a good stir and pour 100ml swiftly into the centre of the pan, in one go. (If you don't have a large ladle, measure it out into a small jug.) Swirl to coat the pan. There will be lacy holes, but don't try to fill them. For crisper edges, add tiny dabs of butter in a few places around the edge. Cook until set and lightly browned around the edge, then loosen gently and flip over and cook on the other side. If the dosa is too delicate to flip without breaking, cook it only on one side, but a good frying pan and spatula should prevent this from happening. Slide out onto a bread board or plate lined with a tea towel and keep warm while you cook the rest. Stir the batter before each use as it settles.

Serve warm with the accompaniments you like, scooped or rolled up. They are thin and delicate, so roll carefully.

CHICKPEA CRÊPES

▲▲▲▲▲▲▲▲▲▲▲▲▲▲▲▲▲▲▲▲

This thin and nutty-tasting crêpe is based on the *Socca* that is a well-known street snack in the south of France. *Socca* is thicker and is cooked on a very wide purpose-made metal plate in the oven. The finished pancake is cut or broken into pieces and sprinkled with salt and pepper before eating. This version is quick and easy, and all you need is a frying pan or pancake pan. Instead of salt and pepper, you could also use spice mixtures such as *za'atar*, *chaat masala*, or a chutney as a dip, accompanied by a nice cold drink. Icing sugar makes a delicious topping for the sweet-toothed, to go with your tea or coffee.

> **MAKES 6–7 CRÊPES (23CM)**

125g gram/chickpea flour (*besan*)
¼–scant ½ tsp salt
scant 325ml water
about 2 tbsp olive oil, for cooking

Sift the gram flour and salt into a bowl. Add the water and whisk to make a thin lump-free batter. Cover with clingfilm and leave for 30 minutes–3 hours.

When ready to cook, stir the batter well. Heat a 23cm frying pan and brush well with oil. Ladle 50–60ml of the batter into the pan and swirl to coat the base. Pour any excess batter back into the bowl. Cook without browning too much on the bottom. Although the brown looks attractive, it gives a slightly bitter aftertaste. Loosen the crêpe with a flexible spatula and flip over to cook briefly on the second side. Fold into quarters and slide out onto a plate. Keep warm while you cook the rest.

Serve with drinks, with the accompaniments described above offered separately. Either give everyone their own with a plate and fork, or cut them up into large pieces and put them on a platter.

GALETTES BRETONNES

▲▲▲▲▲▲▲▲▲▲▲▲▲▲▲▲▲▲▲▲▲▲▲▲

In former days, buckwheat was a godsend to Europeans. It thrived under most conditions and provided welcome nourishment, often in the form of pancakes, such as French *galettes*. A similar pancake exists in Holland, but is thicker and leavened, with the topping – bacon or apples – cooked into the batter. The recipe below is for a *galette complète*, which makes a good breakfast or snack. You can use other toppings, or make them plain and serve as suggested below. If you don't like the nuttiness of buckwheat, use a different crêpe as a base.

> **MAKES 10 GALETTES
> (23–24CM)**

125g plain flour
125g buckwheat flour
generous ¼ tsp salt
½ tsp granulated sugar
1 egg, beaten
250ml milk
250ml lukewarm water
1 tbsp neutral-tasting oil
butter or neutral-tasting oil, for cooking

TOPPING PER *GALETTE*
1 egg
1–2 slices of ham
small handful of shredded tasty cheese,
    such as Gruyère, Emmental,
    Edam, Cheddar
grind of pepper (optional)

Sift the flours together in a large bowl and stir in the salt. Whisk in the egg, milk and about half of the water. Gradually whisk in the rest of the water, followed by 1 tbsp oil, to make a smooth batter. Cover with clingfilm and leave for at least 30 minutes, or refrigerate for several hours. Whisk again before using.

Melt some butter in a 23–24cm frying pan, or brush it with oil. Add about 60ml of the batter and swirl to coat the pan. As soon as the top has set, flip it over. Keep the heat fairly low. Break an egg over the pancake and spread it out. Put the ham in the centre and sprinkle on the cheese and optional black pepper. Once the egg has cooked sufficiently (soft but not raw), fold the sides inwards to make a square parcel, with some filling still visible in the centre. Serve immediately.

Wipe the frying pan clean after each pancake if using butter. Cook the rest in the same way, or make plain and stack them as you cook. Serve warm or cold with icing sugar, butter and lemon juice, or fruit and crème fraîche. A popular variant in France is the *galette saucisse*: a warm sausage wrapped in one of these pancakes.

LATIN AMERICAN CORNMEAL GRIDDLE BREADS
< AREPAS >

▲▲▲▲▲▲▲▲▲▲▲▲▲▲▲▲▲▲▲▲

At a glance, you might mistake them for English muffins, but they are the plump cousins of Mexican corn tortillas. The texture may make them a bit of an acquired taste, but do give them a go. Cornmeal griddle breads with nice crisp crusts and softer but compact insides are a much-loved snack in Latin America. They are made at home or bought from street stalls, stuffed with melting cheese, and/or warm shredded meat, or salads. The 'reina pepiada' given below is a delicious chicken and avocado salad, a Venezuelan speciality. Note that you must use special precooked cornmeal; don't substitute regular cornmeal or tortilla *masa*.

> **MAKES 4 (10CM)**

250g <u>precooked</u> fine white cornmeal
   (*masarepa/harina P.A.N.;* see p.151)
1½ tsp baking powder
¾ tsp salt
2 tsp granulated sugar
2 tbsp neutral-tasting oil, plus extra for
   brushing
about 340ml lukewarm water
Filling suggestions: grated cheese; warm
   shredded meat; chicken or other salads

Put the dry ingredients in a bowl. Add the oil and warm water and use a fork to bring it all together. The porridge-like consistency will change to a soft dough. Knead for 5–6 minutes. Shape into a ball, cover with clingfilm and leave for 15–20 minutes.

Heat a griddle or heavy-based frying pan. Divide the dough into 4 portions and flatten each to a neat 10cm disc. Brush the pan lightly with oil and turn the heat fairly low.

Cook for about 10–13 minutes on each side until crisp and browned in places. They should sound a bit hollow when tapped. Don't undercook, or they will be gummy.

Slice in half, or make a pocket, and fill with cheese and/or warm meat. If using cold salads, cool to at least lukewarm before filling. Serve immediately after filling.

REINA PEPIADA CHICKEN SALAD
For 4 *arepas*, you will need a cooked chicken breast, 1 avocado and 3–4 tbsp mayonnaise. I like to use the chicken from the Shawarma (p.58) or Fajita recipes (p.33) but you can use plain roast chicken too, adding black pepper, etc. to taste. Cut the chicken and avocado into small cubes and mix in the mayonnaise. Adjust the seasonings if necessary. Stuff into 4 *arepas* and there's your *reina pepiada*.

CHAPTER 6
RELISHES & ACCOMPANIMENTS

SALSA FRESCA

This Mexican classic is known by several names: *salsa Mexicana* (what else?), *pico de gallo* (hotly debated by many as *pico de gallo* is also a fruit salad), *salsa bandera* ('flag' salsa; imagine the colours of the Mexican flag and you'll see why) or, most popularly, *salsa fresca* or 'fresh' salsa. Fresh is the word, as it should be served as soon as it is made. The amounts given below make a tasty salsa, but feel free to vary the quantities and flavourings to suit. Don't just keep it for Mexican-inspired food. Its fresh summery flavour goes well with just about anything and it is equally good as a salad on its own.

**MAKES A GARNISH FOR 4
(EASILY DOUBLED)**

250g tasty ripe tomatoes, deseeded
1 red chilli (or a jalapeño),
    deseeded if wished
1 small white onion, chopped medium-fine
small handful of coriander or flat-leaf
    parsley, finely chopped
juice of ½ lime
salt, to taste

Chop the tomatoes into small cubes and put them in a serving bowl. Slice the chilli thinly and add to the bowl along with the other ingredients. Mix well and serve immediately or as soon as possible.

COOKED TOMATO SALSA

Make this salsa in advance and use at room temperature or reheat as needed. I prefer canned chopped tomatoes above the usual fresh, watery supermarket ones. However, if you decide to use fresh tomatoes, choose them with care; you may also need to add a little sugar to balance the acid, along with some salt which is already present in the canned ones.

**SERVES 4
(GENEROUSLY)**

2 tbsp olive oil
1 small onion, finely chopped
2 garlic cloves, crushed
400g can chopped tomatoes
½ tsp dried thyme
¼ tsp dried oregano
¼–½ tsp chilli powder

Heat the oil in a heavy-based pan, add the onion and garlic, and stir-fry until the onion is soft. Add the tomatoes, thyme, oregano and chilli powder and stir well to combine. Reduce the heat and simmer, uncovered, for about 10 minutes. It should have a nice thick consistency. Use warm or at room temperature, as needed.

AVOCADO SALAD

GUACAMOLE

This can be served as a relish or a side dish. In my eyes, it goes with just about anything.

SERVES 4 AS A SIDE DISH
OR MORE AS A RELISH

2 ripe avocados, cubed
1 red chilli, deseeded if wished and
    finely chopped
1 small red onion, finely chopped
1 tbsp finely chopped coriander
juice of 1 lime (or as liked)
    or balsamic vinegar, to taste
salt, to taste

Mix all of the ingredients in a serving bowl. Taste and adjust the salt and tartness if necessary. Cover with clingfilm and leave for a few minutes so that the flavours blend. It can be left for up to an hour or so, but will start to discolour and exude a lot of liquid after that.

Homemade guacamole takes just a few minutes to make and is far tastier than the jars of uniform pea-green paste you can buy in the supermarket. Although it is a typically Mexican accompaniment, it goes very well with lots of other things. Easy canapés: small rounds of good bread topped with guacamole and smoked salmon, or cooked mussels, or prawns, or Serrano-style ham.

MAKES 4 SERVINGS AS A
TORTILLA ACCOMPANIMENT

½–1 lime, or to taste
2 ripe avocados, peeled, stoned and cubed
1 medium tomato, deseeded and chopped
    into tiny pieces
½ a small white onion, finely chopped
¼–½ tsp chilli powder or a good splash of
    hot pepper sauce
1 large garlic clove, crushed
salt, to taste

Squeeze half a lime over the avocado cubes and mash coarsely with a fork. Transfer to a serving bowl. Add the remaining ingredients and mix well. Adjust the seasoning to taste. Cover the bowl with clingfilm and serve as soon as possible after making. If left too long, the guacamole will discolour.

HOT, SWEET & SOUR FRUIT SALAD
< RUJAK OR ROJAK >

▲▲▲▲▲▲▲▲▲▲▲▲▲▲▲▲▲▲▲▲▲

The word *rujak* or *rojak* means 'mixture' and this mixture of fruits is very popular as a snack or ending to a meal in Indonesia, Malaysia and Singapore. A great deal of the charm of *rujak* comes from the contrast of flavours and textures: cool crunchy cucumber, sweet soft pineapple, tangy under-ripe mango, crisp apple finished off with the restrained tartness of tamarind and the searing heat of the chilli. In Indonesia, a fruit called *jambu air* (rose apple) is generally used instead of the apple in this recipe. It is vaguely pear-shaped, with crisp white tart-sweet flesh and a rosy red skin. However, a tartish apple with a red skin will do quite well as a replacement. In Guyana, we had our own drier version, called very succinctly 'mango and salt-and-pepper'. The mango was always green, hard and unripe, sliced and rubbed with salt and chopped bird's-eye chillies: heaven to children and pregnant women.

**MAKES 4 GOOD SERVINGS,
AND WILL SERVE MORE AS A GARNISH**

---

2 tbsp tamarind pulp (see p.153)
60ml hot water
1 red bird's-eye or regular chilli, deseeded
   if wished, and chopped
2 tbsp Demerara or palm sugar
¼ tsp salt
10–15cm piece of cucumber
¼ of a pineapple
1 medium-sized half-ripe mango
1 small fairly tart red-skinned apple
50g roasted peanuts, coarsely crushed or
   chopped (optional)

Put the tamarind pulp, hot water, chilli, sugar and salt in a small food processor or spice grinder and blitz to make a sauce. A mortar and pestle, as used in Asia, is also very effective. Set aside.

Leave the skin on the cucumber for contrast, or peel it if you prefer. Cut it in half lengthways, then into half-moons about 3mm thick. Remove the skin and hard core from the pineapple. Peel the mango and cut off the cheeks and the flesh around the stone. Cut the apple into quarters and remove the core. Slice the pineapple, mango and apple about 5mm thick. (Or you can cut everything, including the cucumber, into small cubes instead.) Put the fruit in a serving bowl, toss with the sauce, sprinkle with peanuts, if using, and serve immediately. If left to stand, liquid will leach out and it will lose some of its crispness.

Serve as a snack, side dish or garnish, for instance with *Martabak* (see p.69).

PERUVIAN ONION RELISH
< SALSA CRIOLLA PERUANA >

▲▲▲▲▲▲▲▲▲▲▲▲▲▲▲▲▲▲▲▲

Continents apart, geographically speaking, but flavour-wise, this simple and tasty Peruvian favourite will pair well with the meatier wraps such as Souvlaki (p.61), Kebab (p.59), Shawarma (p.56) and more. It is usually made with plump local yellow-orange chillies known as *ajíes amarillos*. They are not easy to find outside the region and a green or red chilli will work equally well. Similarly, use parsley or coriander, to suit your taste. Some people hedge their bets and use both.

MAKES 4

1 large red or white onion

1 green or red chilli

juice of 1 small lime

1 tbsp finely chopped flat-leaf parsley or coriander

1 tbsp olive oil

salt, to taste

Peel the onion and cut it in half lengthways. Slice into thin strips about 3–5mm, again lengthways. If using a white onion, rinse it with cold water, drain well and pat dry. This removes some sharpness. Put it in a serving bowl. Cut the chilli in half and discard the membranes and seeds. (Or leave them in if you prefer the kick.) Slice thinly and add to the onion. Mix in the remaining ingredients. Cover and leave at room temperature for a few minutes or up to an hour before serving.

MANGO CHUTNEY

▲▲▲▲▲▲▲▲▲▲▲▲▲▲▲▲▲▲▲▲▲▲▲▲▲▲

Mango chutney is easy to make and, once you have tasted this version, you can adjust the spices to suit for subsequent batches. Do use the seeds – it isn't hard to roast them and they add a lot to the flavour. This is one of the instances where the rock-hard under-ripe mangoes found in Western supermarkets serve a purpose. If your mango is too ripe, the chutney will be too sweet. One very large mango should give you enough flesh, but weigh it after peeling.

MAKES 2 X 375G JARS

generous ½ tsp cumin seeds
generous ½ tsp coriander seeds
generous ¼ tsp fennel seeds
¼ tsp ground cardamom
¼ tsp ground cinnamon
⅛ tsp ground cloves
¼–½ tsp ground cayenne pepper
½ tsp salt
475g flesh from a half-ripe mango
thumb-sized piece of fresh ginger, grated
150g Demerara sugar
150ml water
125ml cider vinegar (or other fruity type)

Put the seeds in a dry frying pan and roast over a medium heat for a few minutes, shaking the pan regularly. They are done when they emit a spicy aroma. Cool, then crush them in a mortar and pestle. Add the remaining spices and mix well. Set aside.

Peel the mango. Cut off the cheeks, the sides and the flesh from around the seed. Slice the pieces just under 5mm thick. Slice again at right angles so that you get chunky matchsticks. Place in a heavy-based pan.

Add the remaining ingredients, and place the pan over a medium-high heat. Bring to the boil, stirring well to combine the ingredients, and at intervals after that. When it comes to the boil, reduce the heat very slightly. From this point on, keep on stirring to prevent it from catching. Cook for about 5 minutes, or until the fruit is very soft. Reduce the heat to low. If you have a stick blender, immerse it in the mixture and whizz briefly until about three-quarters of the fruit turns to pulp. If not, use a potato masher and mash thoroughly, leaving some chunky bits. Increase the heat to medium-high and keep stirring until the mixture is thick. It will take about 10–15 minutes from the time it comes to a boil. To test, pour 1 tsp onto a cold plate. If it barely spreads, the mixture is thick enough. If not, it needs to be cooked a little longer. Ladle the chutney into 2 clean jam jars placed on a folded tea towel. It will thicken slightly as it cools. Cool completely before covering with the lids. Refrigerate the jars; they will keep for about a month in the fridge.

MANGO SALSA

Use this simple salsa as a guideline and vary to suit your taste. You can make it spicier or more tart, and you can choose the type and amount of herbs that you prefer. It goes well with almost any of the wraps and is good with grilled and roasted meats too.

SERVES 4

1 ripe (but still firm) mango
1 small red onion, finely chopped
1 red chilli, deseeded if wished, and sliced
　　or finely chopped
juice of ½–1 lime
1–2 tbsp finely chopped coriander or mint
salt, to taste

Peel the mango and cut off the cheeks, followed by the flesh around the stone. Cut into small dice and put in a serving bowl. Add the other ingredients and mix well. Serve immediately or cover with clingfilm and set aside at room temperature for an hour or two until needed.

CUCUMBER CHUTNEY

CUCUMBER & YOGURT RELISH

This is one of the classic accompaniments for Trinidadian Doubles, a popular street food of curried chickpeas sandwiched between two bara (see p. 21). In Trinidad, a local herb called *chadon béni* (or more colloquially 'shadow bennie') is used and gives a unique flavour. Coriander, or even flat-leaf parsley, will also work. Adjust the chillies to taste, taking their heat into account. Scotch bonnet is extremely hot! Use a light-coloured vinegar, or white balsamic, as dark vinegars spoil the colour.

SERVES 4

1 large cucumber (about 350g)
¾ tsp salt
½ Scotch bonnet chilli, or 1 bird's-eye or regular red chilli, finely chopped
1 large garlic clove, crushed
2 tbsp light-coloured vinegar
small handful of coriander, finely chopped

Peel the cucumber if you prefer. Shred it coarsely on a grater, or cut into very thin matchsticks. Put in a colander placed over a bowl. Sprinkle with the salt and leave for about 10 minutes. Squeeze as much moisture as you can from the cucumber. Put the cucumber in a serving bowl and mix in the other ingredients. Leave at room temperature for an hour before using.

This goes well with spicy meat fillings such as Kebabs (see p.59) and can be used straight away.

SERVES 4

½ large cucumber (about 175g)
1 medium onion, chopped
1 garlic clove, crushed
150g thick Greek-style yogurt
2 tbsp finely chopped mint leaves OR
   2 tbsp finely chopped coriander leaves

Peel the cucumber, cut it into tiny dice (the size of small peas) and put in a bowl. Add the onion and garlic to the cucumber along with the yogurt and chopped herbs. Combine well and cover with clingfilm. Leave at cool room temperature for up to 2 hours or chill until needed. Give it a good stir before using.

QUICK COCONUT CHUTNEY

This is the ideal accompaniment for South Indian *dosas*, and you can pair it with many other things too. Green chilli and lime juice add a fresh crisp note to the sweetness of the coconut, but you can adjust the balance to suit your taste. Traditional coconut chutneys are usually made by roasting fresh coconut over a flame before pounding it with the other ingredients. This 'modern' take is very quick, especially if you use an electric grinder.

SERVES 4 AS A CONDIMENT

50g fine desiccated coconut
½–1 green chilli, deseeded if wished, and
　　thinly sliced
1.5cm piece of fresh ginger, peeled and
　　thinly sliced
about 3 tbsp warm water, or as needed
¼ tsp salt, or to taste
juice of ½ lime, or to taste

Put the coconut in a small dry frying pan over a medium heat. Move it around with a spatula, keeping the sides of the pan clean, as any coconut sticking there will colour more quickly than the rest and burn. Once the coconut starts to colour, things move very fast. When the coconut is almost evenly the colour of Demerara sugar, remove the pan from the heat, stir for 30 seconds and leave to cool slightly.

If you have a small electric grinder/herb chopper or a food processor that can handle small quantities, put all of the ingredients in it and blitz. If not, simply chop the chilli and ginger finely and crush thoroughly with the other ingredients in a mortar and pestle. If the mixture is a little too wet, add 1–2 tsp of coconut; if it is too dry, add a little more water. Add extra salt and lime juice as desired. It should have a pleasantly tart undertone, and some people even like it to be downright sour. That's up to you – and the particular lime you use, as acidity level is not standard in any fruit.

Put into a small bowl and serve immediately, or cover with clingfilm and chill until needed. Give it a stir before serving and add a little more water if necessary. Eat within a day or two.

KIMCHI-STYLE CUCUMBER PICKLE

Kimchi is a Korean staple that is made from fermented vegetables, such as cabbage and cucumber, and a variety of seasonings including a generous amount of chilli. You can buy it in jars from Asian grocers, but for a quick(ish)-fix approximation, this cucumber pickle works well. Use it with *Bulgogi* (see p.28) and other meats.

SERVES 4 (GENEROUSLY)

1 large cucumber (about 350g)
1 generous tsp salt
½ medium carrot
1 spring onion
2 garlic cloves
thumb-sized piece of fresh ginger
1 tbsp granulated sugar
1–2 tsp chilli flakes
2 tbsp rice vinegar
2 tsp fish sauce
1 tbsp Japanese-style soy sauce

Cut the cucumber into coarse matchsticks, about 2–3cm long and put them in a colander. Sprinkle with the salt and toss it up to distribute the salt. Allow to rest on a plate or in the sink for about 20 minutes.

Meanwhile, cut the carrot and spring onion into thin matchsticks, the same length as the cucumber. Put them in a large bowl. Slice the garlic and ginger paper thin and add to the bowl along with the other ingredients. Give the colander a good shake to get rid of excess liquid and add the cucumber to the bowl. Toss everything well together and transfer to a non-reactive bowl with a well-sealing lid. Chill for at least 8 hours, but preferably overnight, and bring to room temperature before serving.

Best eaten within 24 hours. It will taste good for a day or two, but a lot of liquid will seep out, making it less appetising.

YOGURT & GARLIC SAUCE

GARLIC SAUCE
< TOUM >

This is the ideal accompaniment for Courgette & Feta Cakes (see p.95). Yogurt is a much-loved ingredient in Turkish cuisine and finds its way into soups, stews and snacks of all kinds, as well as simple but tasty dressings such as the following one. The word itself was borrowed from the Turks, who are credited with having introduced yogurt to the Western world. Turkish yogurt is similar in consistency to the better-known thick Greek kind.

This smooth and mild-tasting garlic sauce goes well with almost any Middle Eastern or Asian-style wrap and is an essential component for a Chicken Shawarma (see p.56). The traditional but tedious and endless hand-pounding is a thing of the past for most people, although some say that it is the only way to create the right consistency. Use a blender that can handle the small quantity effectively, or even better – a stick blender.

SERVES 4

SERVES 4

200g thick Greek-style yogurt
1 large garlic clove, finely crushed
1–2 tbsp finely chopped mint or dill
salt and freshly ground black pepper (optional)

Simply stir all of the ingredients together in a suitable bowl. Cover with clingfilm and set aside.

5–6 firm garlic cloves
¼ tsp salt
100ml neutral-tasting oil, such as groundnut, or corn
1 tbsp lemon juice

Crush the garlic with the salt in a mortar and pestle. Put them in a blender that can handle small quantities or transfer to a tall narrow container that will hold a stick blender. Add 2 tsp oil and switch on the blender. Keep on adding oil by the tsp, with the motor running. When you have added half of the oil, start adding lemon juice a few drops at a time, alternating with the oil. Blend well between additions and only add more liquids when the previous addition has been well incorporated. It is ready when it has the consistency of apple sauce.

TAMARIND SAUCE

You will find this spicy, sweet and sour sauce in places as far apart as Southeast Asia and the Caribbean. In Guyana, we mainly eat it with fritters and Indian flatbreads. In Southeast Asia, it is a popular accompaniment for fish cakes. If you can get good-quality tamarind pulp or paste, use it. All too often, the commercial pastes look like diluted tar and taste of nothing in particular. A block of pressed 'wet' tamarind, bought from an Asian shop, will keep for months in the fridge and you can make your own flavourful paste as needed. (See below.)

SERVES 4

2 tbsp thick tamarind pulp (see below)
1 packed tsp cornflour
150ml water
1 bird's-eye chilli, deseeded if wished, and very finely chopped
1 garlic clove, grated or very finely crushed
1 tbsp rice or cider vinegar
½ tsp salt
2–3 tsp granulated sugar, or as needed

For the pulp, put a large knob of tamarind in a small bowl and pour over about 3 tbsp boiling water. How large depends on if there are seeds or not; without seeds, about the size of a large walnut, or a small egg if it has seeds. Press with a fork so that the water comes into contact with as much of the fruit as possible. Leave for a few minutes. Massage the tamarind with your fingers through a sieve, onto a plate or bowl. Scrape the pulp off the outside of the sieve. You should have about 2 tbsp of thick tamarind pulp.

Dissolve the cornflour in a little of the water. Put all of the ingredients in a small pan. Bring to the boil while stirring with a small whisk. Let bubble for about 2 minutes, still stirring with the whisk. It should thicken slightly. Remove from the heat and taste. If necessary, add a little more sugar. Allow to cool. It will keep for a few days in the fridge in a clean screw-topped jar. Serve at room temperature in individual dipping bowls.

NUOC CHAM

▲▲▲▲▲▲▲▲▲▲▲▲▲▲▲▲▲▲▲▲▲▲▲▲

This simple Vietnamese dipping sauce is served with dishes such as Crystal (Summer) Rolls (see p.30). It is very easy to make and will bring a burst of flavour to whatever you dip in it. Use bird's-eye or long chillies in an amount to suit your taste. You can keep this in a closed jar in the fridge for a day or two, but it is so easy to make that you can just whip it up as needed.

SERVES 4

1 garlic clove, crushed
½–1 red chilli, finely chopped
2 tbsp granulated sugar
2 tbsp lime juice
4 tbsp fish sauce (*nuoc mam*)
4 tbsp water
2 tsp rice vinegar
few thin slices of the green part of
    a spring onion, to garnish

Combine the ingredients in a jug and stir well to dissolve the sugar. When ready to serve, spoon it out into small dipping bowls, making sure that some of the chilli is in each bowl too. Sprinkle the spring onion over the top and serve with Crystal Rolls (see p.30) or other similar dishes.

SIMPLE PEANUT SAUCE

▲▲▲▲▲▲▲▲▲▲▲▲▲▲▲▲▲▲▲▲▲▲▲▲▲▲

Thanks to Holland's colonial past, this Indonesian sauce is now mainstream Dutch and people will eat it equally happily with satay or chips. The base can be bought in powdered form or in a jar – a kind of seasoned peanut butter – but it is very easy to make using regular peanut butter too. It will go with satay and barbecued meats and can be spooned onto many Asian-style wraps such as Crystal Rolls (p.30) and Fresh Lumpia (p.26). Use the smaller amount of liquid for a thick sauce, or the larger amount for a thinner one. It thickens as it cools and can be further diluted with hot water if necessary. You may also omit the cumin and ground coriander.

> SERVES 4 AS A DIPPING SAUCE OR CONDIMENT
> (DOUBLE IT FOR CHICKEN SATAY (P.46)
> IF YOU LIKE LOTS OF SAUCE)

75g smooth natural (no added sugar) peanut butter
100–125ml water or coconut milk
1 tbsp cider vinegar (or other fruity type)
1 tbsp Japanese-style soy sauce
½–1 red chilli, finely chopped
1 garlic clove, crushed
¼ tsp ground cumin (optional)
¼ tsp ground coriander (optional)
1 spring onion, finely chopped
handful of chopped peanuts (optional)

Put all of the ingredients, except the spring onion and peanuts, if using, into a small pan and bring to the boil while stirring continuously with a small whisk. Let bubble for about a minute or two; it will thicken. Remove from the heat and stir in the spring onion, along with the chopped peanuts, if using. Serve warm or at room temperature, in a single bowl or individual ones.

REFRIED BEANS

Refried beans are in fact first boiled and then fried just once, not twice as the name implies. Mexican families will cook large pots of beans and use them in various ways, such as this. Boil your own beans in the usual way or use canned beans if you prefer. Just make sure that they are cooked very soft.

SERVES 4

250g cooked black or pinto beans
3 tbsp olive oil
1 small onion, finely chopped
1 garlic clove, crushed
¼ tsp ground cumin
¼ tsp chilli powder
75–100ml stock, such as from Shredded
  Beef Tacos recipe (p.36) or water,
  or as needed
salt, if needed

If using canned beans, rinse and drain.

Heat the oil in a non-stick pan, add the onion and garlic, and stir-fry until soft. Add the spices, followed by the beans. Stir to combine and add 75ml stock or water. Mash the simmering beans coarsely with a wooden spoon or more thoroughly with a potato masher. Keep on adding tbsp of liquid as needed and remove from the heat as soon as you have the right texture. It should be on the mushy side as it will thicken and dry out a bit while it stands. Taste and add salt if needed.

Use warm or at room temperature with Burritos (p.34) and other Mexican-style dishes.

CHAPTER 7
SWEET SUGGESTIONS

WALNUT CREAM CRÊPES WITH CHOCOLATE SAUCE
< GUNDEL PALACSINTA >

▲▲▲▲▲▲▲▲▲▲▲▲▲▲▲▲▲▲▲▲▲▲

When Károly Gundel opened the doors of his restaurant in Budapest in 1910, it quickly became a haunt for the top layers of society. To this day, Gundel's remains the most famous restaurant in Hungary. These sumptuous pancakes, one of Károly's creations, continue to titillate the taste buds of discerning diners and have been endlessly copied by others. You can cook and fill them several hours beforehand, reheating just before serving.

MAKES 8 (SERVES 4)

8 x 23–24cm Crepes made with sparkling water (p.23)
½ quantity (or more!) of the filling for Chocolate Roulade (see p.146), warmed, with 1 tbsp rum stirred through

FILLING
150g walnuts
100g caster sugar
¾ tsp ground cinnamon
200ml double cream
1–2 tbsp rum
finely grated zest of 1 orange

Start preparing the filling while the crêpe batter is resting. Put the walnuts, sugar and cinnamon in a food processor and grind as finely as you can. Heat the cream in a small pan until almost boiling. Reduce the heat and stir in the ground walnuts along with the rum and orange zest. Cook over a low heat for 3–4 minutes, stirring gently. The mixture should be a thinly spreadable paste which will thicken to the consistency of soft peanut butter as it cools. Set aside until needed. If it thickens too much while standing, add a few drops of cream as needed.

Cook the crepes as directed on p.23 and leave them flat on the plate. **For triangles,** spread 2 tbsp of the filling over half of a crêpe. Fold it over, then fold again so that it is a quarter of its original shape. **For rolls,** spread the filling in a 10cm band along the middle of a crêpe, going all the way to the top and bottom. Fold one side inwards over the filling, then roll up to form a cylinder. Transfer to a platter and keep warm or allow to cool, depending on when you will serve them.

When you are ready to serve, reheat the crêpes on the platter in the microwave, covered with kitchen paper; or cover with foil and reheat in a slow oven (about 140°C/Gas Mark 1). Transfer 2 per person to warmed plates, and spoon some of the sauce over the crêpes to serve.

CRÊPES SUZETTE

▲▲▲▲▲▲▲▲▲▲▲▲▲▲▲▲▲▲▲▲▲▲▲▲

This classic French dessert comes in many forms, from simple crêpes doused with Grand Marnier to complicated versions with fillings and sauces, and they can even be flambéed at the table for special effect. My version is quite straightforward. They are scrumptious eaten straight from the stove, but the reheated ones have a charm all their own as well.

**MAKES 12 CRÊPES
(SERVES ABOUT 4)**

1 recipe Crêpes (see p.23) (See note below)

SAUCE
75g butter
grated zest of scant 1 orange
50g granulated sugar
60ml orange juice
40ml Grand Marnier

Make the crêpes as directed on p.23.

For the sauce, put the butter in a small pan and add the remaining ingredients. Heat slowly to melt the butter, stirring to combine to a smooth sauce, then simmer for 5 minutes. Set aside until needed and reheat briefly if the butter sets.

To reheat, have warmed plates and a warmed dish standing by. Heat 2 tbsp of the orange sauce in a frying pan. Place 4 folded crêpes in the pan so that together they form a whole circle. Drizzle with 1 generous tbsp of the sauce. Warm through completely or even leave them in a little longer for some caramelisation. This is absolutely delicious, but will make the crêpes crisp. Turn them over and warm on the second side. Transfer to the serving dish and keep warm. Repeat the process, warming a second batch of 4 crêpes followed by the last batch. Add any leftover sauce to the pan after removing the last crêpes and drizzle it over the crêpes in the serving dish. Serve immediately on the warmed plates with orange segments or slices, if liked. And really, if you just want to reheat the folded crêpes in the microwave and drizzle warm sauce over them, I won't even try to stop you. Just enjoy them.

Note: Use only milk for the crêpes and add 2 tsp Grand Marnier, along with a large pinch of orange zest, to the batter. Use the rest of the zest for the sauce. Fold the cooked crêpes into quarters and keep warm, or cool and reheat later. If serving them straight away, have the sauce standing by. Drizzle a few tbsp of the warm sauce over each serving.

SIMPLE SYRUP

This syrup can be used for moistening the filo pastries and is also a useful standby for other purposes such as fruit salads, cakes and even cocktails. It will keep in an airtight container in the fridge for several weeks. The syrup can be optionally flavoured with rosewater or orange blossom water, depending on what you use it for.

MAKES JUST OVER 400ML

375g granulated sugar
280ml water
1½ tsp strained lemon juice
rosewater or orange blossom water
   (optional), to taste

Put the sugar, water and lemon juice in a heavy-based pan over a medium heat. Bring to the boil while stirring to dissolve the sugar. Reduce the heat and simmer for 5 minutes. Remove from the heat and allow to cool. If using, stir rosewater or orange blossom water into the cold syrup, a few drops at a time, until you get the desired flavour.

SPONGE PANCAKES & CREAM HALF MOONS
< BEGHRIR & KATAYEF >

These spongy pancakes are often eaten to break the fast during Ramadan in Muslim and Arab countries. In Morocco, they like them topped with melted butter and honey and call them *beghrir*. Others prefer a sweet cheese or cream-filled version called *katayef*, not to be confused with the thread pastry known as *katayif* or *kadayif*. The *katayef* are folded into half moons, or pinched into cones. Sometimes the half moons are sealed completely and deep-fried before serving. They are irresistible in all their forms.

MAKES 12

PANCAKES
125g very fine semolina
125g plain flour
1¼ tsp easy-blend dried yeast
¾ tsp baking powder
¼ tsp salt
1 tsp granulated sugar
1 egg, beaten
315ml tepid water
neutral-tasting oil, for brushing

FILLING
35g icing sugar, sifted
350g ricotta
about 60g pistachios, finely chopped

For the pancakes, mix the dry ingredients together in a bowl. Add the liquids and whisk well for about 5 minutes until very smooth. Cover the bowl with clingfilm and leave in a warm place for about 1 hour, or until the batter increases in volume and becomes frothy on the surface.

Heat a griddle or heavy-based frying pan. Reduce the heat and brush with oil. Stir the batter gently from the bottom to re-incorporate what may have settled, but don't beat too much air out. Use a 50ml ladle to pour a portion of batter into the pan. It should spread out of its own accord and develop lots of little holes. Cook on one side only. It is ready when the top shows no wetness. Keep the cooked pancakes wrapped in a tea towel so that they remain flexible. If filling, allow to cool.

For the filling, whisk the icing sugar thoroughly into the ricotta. When you are ready to serve, put 1 heaped tbsp of this on one half of a pancake and spread it out so that it nearly comes to the edge of that half. Fold over, but don't bring the top all the way to the edge. Leave almost 1cm of filling showing around the edge. Sprinkle chopped pistachios over the visible filling and serve immediately.

PISTACHIO & CREAM PARCELS

Katmer is the traditional Turkish treat to follow a good kebab. Properly speaking, *katmer* is quite large (about 20cm square) and is fried or baked as you wait. *Kaymak* is thick Turkish cream, sold in cans in some Middle Eastern shops; crème fraîche is a good substitute. Eat them slightly warm or at room temperature.

MAKES 12

40g butter, melted, plus extra for greasing
125g pistachios, finely ground
50g granulated sugar
100g crème fraîche or *kaymak*
6 sheets of filo pastry, 25 x 25cm
   OR 2 sheets, about 50 x 36cm
150ml prepared cold Simple Syrup, or to
   taste (see p.137)

Lightly grease a small baking sheet. Combine the pistachios, sugar and crème fraîche in a bowl.

If using filo sheets 25 x 25cm, cut them in half to make 12 rectangles, 12.5 x 25cm. If using sheets 50 x 36cm, cut them into 3 strips 12cm wide and cut these in half. You will have 12 rectangles 12 x 25cm.

Place a rectangle of filo on your work surface, short sides at the top and bottom. Keep the rest covered. Put 1 generous tbsp of the filling about 3cm from the bottom (a short side). Bring the bottom edge up over the filling and fold the long sides inwards so that they meet in the middle. Brush with melted butter. Fold the package over loosely, 'wrapping' it in itself until you reach the end, to create a square pastry. Place it on the baking sheet and shape the rest in the same way.

Brush the squares lightly with any leftover butter. They can be prepared up to this stage and left covered at cool room temperature or in the fridge for a few hours, to be baked as needed.

Preheat the oven to 180°C/Gas Mark 4, and bake for about 15 minutes until golden brown and crisp.

Crowd the hot pastries together on the baking sheet and pour the cold syrup evenly over them. Turn them over after 3–4 minutes, leave them for a minute or two, then re-invert. Serve warm or at room temperature.

BANANA SPRING ROLLS
< TURRON >

▲▲▲▲▲▲▲▲▲▲▲▲▲▲▲▲▲▲▲▲▲▲

Hmmm.... isn't *turron* a kind of Spanish nougat? Quite right, *turrón* is. But in the Philippines, where many Spanish food traditions have been either replicated or transformed into local variations, they are delicious banana spring rolls. *Turrons* are widely sold by street vendors and in school canteens where some cooks sprinkle extra sugar onto the roll or drop a little into the oil. This is meant to produce a nice caramelisation, but in my experience it only serves to create a great big mess while cooking. The bananas must be of the cooking kind: plantains, or they will become mushy while frying. If your supermarket does not stock them, try a Caribbean or Asian grocery store. They should not be hard to get hold of. This is the perfect way of using up a packet of wrappers, and you can make as many or as few as you like. They are usually eaten plain, but if you wanted to dip them in some of the chocolate sauce from the Gundel Pancakes (see p.134), I would be the last person to stop you.

MAKES 8

2–3 large ripe plantains (cooking bananas)
8 spring roll wrappers, about 20 x 20cm
1 egg white, loosely whisked
about 4 tbsp light or dark soft brown sugar
neutral-tasting oil, for deep-frying

Peel the plantains and cut them in half. Cut each half into 3–4 slices, about 1cm thick and 10cm long. The number of slices per plantain will depend on its size and length.

Lay a wrapper in a diamond shape on your work surface, i.e. with the points falling at the points of the compass. Brush the edges of the wrapper with egg white. Put a slice of plantain horizontally on the wrapper, about 5cm above the bottom point. Sprinkle ½ tsp of sugar over it. Fold the bottom point over the plantain, then fold the sides of the

wrapper inwards over the plantain. Roll up neatly to form a flat roll. Brush the point with more egg white before pressing it to seal. Shape the others in the same way.

Heat enough oil for deep-frying in a suitable pan to about 180°C/350°F, or until a cube of bread browns in 30 seconds. Deep-fry the rolls until crisp and light golden brown. The plantain should be cooked through. Remove and drain on kitchen paper. Allow to cool for a few minutes before serving so that the plantain does not burn your mouth.

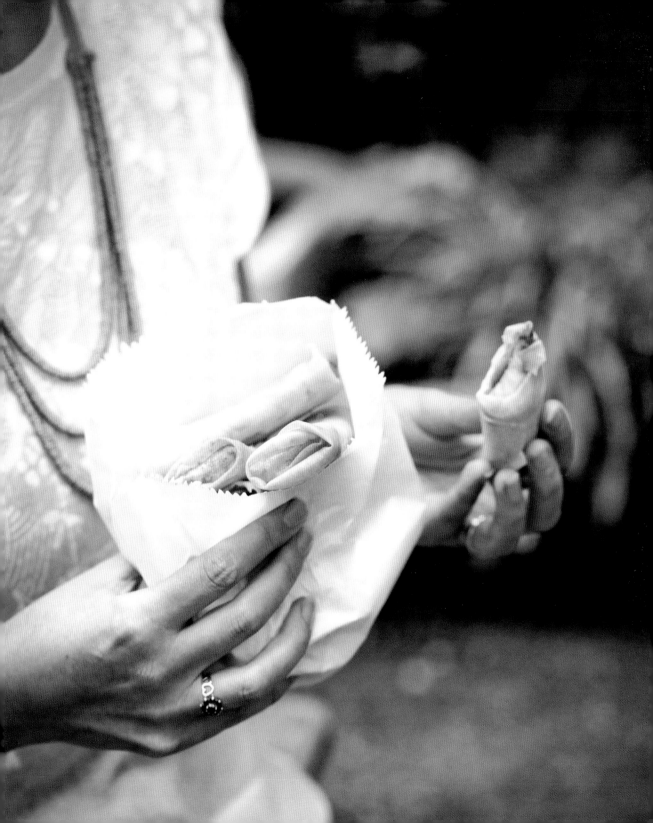

CINNAMON & WALNUT GRIDDLE CAKES

In Indian households the last piece of *roti* dough is often used to make a 'sugar roti' as a treat. The melting sugar always manages to find a weak part in the thin dough, creating a delicious caramelised effect as well as a huge mess. When I saw the Korean dough cakes *hoddeok*, with a sugar and walnut filling, I decided to marry the two into this hybrid. Eaten fresh from the pan, they are crisp on the outside, with a chewy softness on the inside that is a little like the texture of a bagel. You can reheat leftovers in the toaster next day, say for breakfast.

MAKES 8 (ABOUT 8CM)

250g plain flour, plus extra for dusting
2 tsp baking powder
¼ tsp salt
1 tsp granulated sugar
1 tbsp neutral-tasting oil
about 150ml lukewarm water
butter, for cooking

FILLING
3 tbsp sugar (white or brown)
¾ tsp ground cinnamon
35g walnuts

Sift the flour, baking powder and salt into a bowl. Add the sugar, oil and enough water to make a very soft dough. Knead for 2–3 minutes. It will still look quite shaggy and rough-looking. Shape into a ball, put in the bowl and cover with clingfilm. Leave at room temperature for 10 minutes.

For the filling, put the sugar, cinnamon and walnuts in a small food processor and pulse in bursts until the walnuts are very fine.

Re-knead the dough lightly until smooth. Divide into 8 portions and dust with flour. Flatten one between your palms to make a 10cm disc. Pinch the rim to make it thinner than the rest, or the seal-side will be too thick. Hold the disc in your cupped hand and pour 1 good tbsp of the filling into the centre. Pinch to seal into a ball and lay it seal-side down on a floured work surface. Shape 3 more in the same way before starting to cook them.

Heat a small knob of butter in a non-stick pan. Put in the 4 balls, seam-side down, and cook over a medium heat for about 1 minute. Flip over and use a wide spatula to quickly and carefully flatten each cake to a diameter of about 8cm. Cook on both sides, turning as necessary, until golden brown and cooked through.

Shape the remaining cakes while the first batch is cooking. Cook in the same way. Eat warm.

CHOCOLATE ROULADE

This is not your usual Swiss roll. The cake layer is pancake-thin, and gives a very attractive spiral pattern that seems to go on and on....

MAKES 1

CAKE
75g butter, softened, plus extra for greasing
100g plain flour
scant ¼ tsp salt
¼ tsp baking powder
3 eggs, separated
50g + 100g caster sugar
1 tsp vanilla extract
50ml milk

FILLING
200ml double cream
200g dark chocolate (50–70% cocoa solids), finely chopped

Grease 2 baking sheets, about 28 x 38cm or slightly smaller. Line the base neatly with baking parchment. Preheat the oven to 200°C/Gas Mark 6.

Start with the filling. Put the cream in a small pan and bring to the boil. Remove from the heat and add the chocolate. Give the pan a shake so that all of the chocolate is covered with cream. Leave for a minute or two and then stir gently until the chocolate and cream are well combined. Set aside.

Sift the flour with the salt and baking powder. In a scrupulously clean bowl, whisk the egg whites until foaming. Add the 50g sugar in a slow stream, while still whisking. Continue to whisk to soft peaks. Set aside.

In a second bowl, mix the butter with the remaining sugar. Add the egg yolks and vanilla extract, and beat until the mixture is smooth and creamy. Gently fold in half of the egg whites. Fold in half of the flour, followed by the rest of the whites and the remaining flour. Gently mix in the milk.

Divide the batter between the 2 baking sheets and level it carefully. The edges should be as thick as the rest, or they will become crisp and will have to be cut off, losing some cake.

Bake for about 5 minutes. The cakes should barely colour. Turn 1 sheet out onto a work surface lined with a sheet of clingfilm. Turn the second one out onto the first, leaving the parchment in place on both. Cover with another sheet of clingfilm until needed.

Line another part of the work surface with enough clingfilm to easily hold the 2 cake layers side by side, short ends joined. Put the cakes on it, short sides together, and trim away any hard bits if necessary.

Now on to the rolling. The filling should be fairly liquid for this method: spread three-quarters of the filling over the whole surface of 1 cake and half of the next one. With the aid of the clingfilm, roll up from the covered short side, as neatly as you can. The filling will flow forwards as you roll and will end up covering the rest of the cake. If there are bald spots, use some of the reserved filling to fill them. If the filling has thickened too much to flow, you will need to spread it with a palette knife over the entire surface of the cake. Once rolled, put the roulade seam-side down onto a plate lined with clingfilm and glaze all over the outside surface with the remaining filling. Chill until well set.

To serve, slice very thinly (5mm) with a large sharp knife held under hot running water and dried immediately. Warm and dry the knife before every cut. If wished, a dusting of cocoa powder or icing sugar gives a nice decorative touch. Keep uneaten portions refrigerated.

ALMOND FLUTES
< FLOGERES ME AMIGDALA >

▲▲▲▲▲▲▲▲▲▲▲▲▲▲▲▲▲▲▲▲▲▲▲

These luscious Greek pastries are easy to make and you can adjust the amount of syrup to suit your taste. As the filling contains some sugar, they are quite good without syrup too, with a dusting of icing sugar. In that case, allow them to cool on a wire rack and dust with the sugar just before serving.

MAKES 12

3 large sheets of filo pastry, 50 x 36cm
  OR 12 pre-cut ones, 25 x 25cm
125g butter, melted, plus extra for greasing
100–175ml prepared cold Simple Syrup, to
  taste (see p.137)

FILLING
125g finely ground almonds
2 tbsp fine semolina
2 egg yolks
100m double cream
50g granulated sugar
large pinch of grated lemon zest (optional)

Make the filling first. Combine all of the ingredients for the filling and mix to a smooth paste. Set aside for at least 1 hour to give the semolina time to swell properly, or it will burst through the pastry while baking.

If using the larger filo sheets, cut with scissors to make 12 rectangles, about 25 x 18cm. Stack them and keep covered with clingfilm. Preheat the oven to 180°C/Gas Mark 4. Lightly grease a small baking sheet.

Place 1 sheet of filo on your work surface. If using the self-cut rectangles, position them so that the narrow sides are left and right. Brush with melted butter. Place 1 generous tbsp of filling near the bottom of the sheet, leaving about 4cm free at the base and 6cm at each side. Use the spoon to help shape it into a rough sausage. Fold the bottom flap over the filling. Fold the 2 sides inwards over the filling. They should just touch in the middle. Roll up the pastry loosely but neatly and place on the baking sheet. Use up the rest of the sheets in the same way.

Brush the flutes with any remaining butter and bake for about 25 minutes until crisp and golden brown.

As soon as you remove the baking sheet from the oven, crowd them together on the sheet and pour the cold syrup over them. Allow to cool, then remove from the syrup and drain on a wire rack. They will keep at cool room temperature for up to 3 days, but will obviously be crispest on the day of baking. They can also be frozen.

APPLE TURNOVERS
< APPELFLAPPEN >

▲▲▲▲▲▲▲▲▲▲▲▲▲▲▲▲▲▲▲▲▲

Although anyone can make these apple turnovers in next to no time, this doesn't make them less popular as a bakery item in Holland and they literally fly across the counter, especially when still warm from the baker's oven. Usually eaten with coffee, they are also excellent served warm with ice cream or crème fraîche as a dessert. They are best eaten fresh from the oven, as they soften if left to stand, so halve the recipe if that suits your situation better.

MAKES 8

8 squares of ready-made puff pastry, about 13 x 13cm or thereabouts
butter, for greasing
2 large apples, peeled and cored (about 400g)
40g granulated sugar, plus extra granulated sugar, the coarser the better, for sprinkling
1 tsp ground cinnamon
1½ tbsp cornflour
40g sultanas
beaten egg, for glazing

If using frozen pastry, allow it to thaw properly. Preheat the oven to 200°C/Gas Mark 6. Grease a baking sheet lightly.

For the filling, slice the apples about 5mm thick and chop roughly. Mix the apples, sugar, cinnamon, cornflour and sultanas together in a bowl. With your eye, divide the pastry square into 2 triangles and put a portion of filling on 1 triangle. Moisten a fingertip with water and run it around the edge of the pastry square. Fold over into a triangular shape and press the edges together. Crimp the edges with a fork to seal. Arrange on the baking sheet, brush the tops with beaten egg, then prick each pastry with a fork in 3 or 4 places. Use a small spoon to sprinkle the coarse granulated sugar generously and neatly over the triangles.

Bake for 15–20 minutes, until crisp and golden brown. Eat warm or at room temperature.

INGREDIENTS

SALT

Salt is a very personal thing and I tend to be quite cautious with it. While you can always add more afterwards, it is next to impossible to rescue an over-salted dish. Use salt to your own liking in the recipes, with my amounts as a guideline. Unless otherwise stated, salt refers to fine table salt.

READY-MADE WRAPPERS

Dried rice paper rounds for Crystal Rolls (see p.30) and the like are sold in packs, in various diameters. They simply need to be moistened, as directed in the recipe. Spring roll and gyoza dumpling wrappers can be found in the freezer section of some good supermarkets, and if not, certainly in the freezer of a Chinese or other Asian shop. These need to be properly thawed before use. Once thawed, they will keep for a few days in the fridge. Rewrap them well. Flour tortillas are so easy to make, and taste so much better than bought ones, that I encourage you very enthusiastically to try your hand (p.8).

FATS AND OILS

I use unsalted butter, so if you only have salted butter to hand, make the necessary adjustments with the salt in the recipe. When the choice is given between butter or oil, say for frying pancakes, it is purely up to you.

Butter is, of course, more flavourful and richer-tasting. Ghee is clarified butter and is a great favourite in Indian cooking. It has a lower moisture content than butter and will not brown and burn as fast, nor is it prone to spitting. Although I am normally a great advocate of natural fats, there are cases when vegetable shortening is a better alternative than butter. I ask for it only when it really makes a difference to the result. This will always be in texture, as shortening has no flavour of its own. It usually comes as a solid but soft white fat, in a pack or tub. On the positive side, good shortening manufacturers appear to have eliminated trans fats from the ingredients.

Groundnut, corn, sunflower and canola oils are all neutral-tasting and will not dominate. You can use them interchangeably, although my preference is groundnut oil. They are suitable for both shallow- and deep-frying. Olive oil has a more pronounced flavour and a lower smoking point and will always be specifically asked for in a recipe when needed.

FLOURS

Strong flour (bread flour) has a higher percentage of gluten than plain flour. Gluten develops when a dough is kneaded well. The dough becomes elastic and gives the typical texture we expect from bread. Strong flour also absorbs more liquid than plain flour. For these reasons, interchanging flour types in the recipes will affect the outcome.

Semolina is milled from durum wheat, a hard type of wheat that is also used for bread flours. For semolina, the wheat is broken down into fine, medium or coarse particles, instead of being ground to flour. All have their specific uses. Fine semolina is used in this book; it adds a little bite to the texture, but still combines well with the other ingredients.

Cornmeal is made from finely ground corn kernels. I use the fine kind that you would normally use for making polenta. Cornflour, on the other hand, is rightly called 'cornstarch' by the Americans. That is exactly what it is: the starch from corn kernels. It is used to 'cut' flour to give a more tender texture, or as a binding agent in sauces and batters. One recipe uses *masarepa*. This is a precooked cornmeal, usually white, that is used in some Latin American countries, such as Venezuela. It is not manufactured or prepared in the same way as Mexican *masa harina*, and the two are not interchangeable. The brand P.A.N. (not to be confused with the Spanish word '*pan*' that means bread) is widely available and people sometimes simply refer to *masarepa* as '*harina P.A.N*'. I have not used *masa harina* in any recipes because I find it almost impossible to buy in Europe.

Rice flour in this book always means the 'regular' (i.e. non-glutinous) kind that is usually sold simply as 'rice flour' in Western supermarkets. Glutinous rice flour will give a completely different – chewy and gummy – result and must be used differently.

Buckwheat flour has a pleasantly nutty taste and a slightly sticky texture. If your supermarket does not stock it, look in a health food shop.

Chickpea flour or gram flour is often labelled by its Indian name '*besan*'. Another nutty flour, it is equally at home in sweet and savoury preparations. Asian grocers have a rapid turnover, so it will generally be quite fresh.

YEAST

Easy-blend dried yeast (also called instant) is used in this book. It cannot be replaced, weight for weight, with other kinds such as regular (coarser) dried yeast or fresh compressed yeast. The joy of easy-blend dried yeast is that the grains are very fine and can be mixed into the dry ingredients without having to be re-animated beforehand in warm liquid. And on this topic: yeast is a living organism and needs to be treated as such. Err on the side of cooler liquids rather than boiling ones. It reacts best and quickest to blood-temperature liquids (37°C/98.6°F). Liquids that are extremely hot will kill off cells instead of encouraging them to multiply in a comfortable atmosphere. If the liquid is cooler than blood temperature, it will simply take longer for the dough to rise. Always check the 'sell-by' date and use opened packets quickly, even if they haven't reached the date.

EGGS

My eggs weigh about 55g in the shell and 50g out of it. These are the ones that are usually called medium or standard in most countries. A few grams here or there will not make a major difference to the outcome, but can sometimes mean a stickier, runnier or drier consistency than intended. Try to stick to this size to avoid having to make alterations to the recipe.

CHEESE

The cheeses suggested are intended as an indication and can be substituted at your discretion. Cheeses for grating and shredding must be firm enough. They should be tasty and mature, with good softening and melting properties. Cheddar, Gouda, Comté and similar cheeses will all work. Note that shredded cheese is coarser than grated cheese. It comes out in thin strips, retaining more texture than cheese that has been grated.

GARAM MASALA AND CURRY POWDER

Both are preblended dry spice mixtures. Although the actual components and proportions will vary from brand to brand, it should not affect the outcome of a recipe. Curry powder, popular in Caribbean cooking, takes most of its colour from the turmeric in the blend. It is sharp-tasting and should never be used raw. Garam masala is a mixture of sweeter, more aromatic spices and is used in smaller quantities, usually to complement curry powder.

CHILLIES

Fresh chillies can vary not only from variety to variety, but also within a variety itself. It's the luck of the draw. Sometimes an ordinary long red chilli will leave you gasping for breath and at other times you will be left waiting for the kick that never comes. And of course, people's heat thresholds vary greatly. The heat is in the seeds and membranes, so remove those if you prefer. When just 'chilli' is stated, I normally use the common long chillies that you can buy just about anywhere. Green (unripe) chillies have a different flavour to red ones and are characteristic of some dishes. Bird's-eye chillies are tiny, about 2–3cm long, but contain all the heat – and sometimes more – of their bigger brothers. Scotch bonnet is very similar to habañero and will blow your brains out if not used with care. In Guyana we call them 'ball o' fire'; draw your own conclusion.

Dried chillies can also vary in strength, but more importantly: be aware that the measures for chilli flakes and chilli powder are not interchangeable. Flakes take up far less room in a measuring spoon than powder, so if a recipe calls for 1 tsp of flakes and you substitute 1 tsp of powder, you will be increasing the heat dramatically. Powder will give an even result, but flakes add a little excitement as you never know where that seed is lurking.

FRESH HERBS

Bear in mind that 'handfuls' are an average woman's hand, my own being the reference point. Dill, coriander and parsley are used in many of the recipes, and mint in a few. I use flat-leaf parsley, which is full of flavour and doesn't leave irritating bits at the back of your throat the way curly parsley can. Dill and coriander, in particular, can vary in strength, and I find that this has a bearing to the source. When I buy them from an ethnic greengrocer they are far stronger (and far cheaper) than when I buy them from a mainstream Dutch greengrocer or supermarket. There is nothing you can do about it, and I don't plan to send you scouring the area for strong herbs. Just know that this happens and make any necessary adjustments – upwards or downwards – to suit your taste.

GINGER

Its shape makes a 'thumb' an easy measuring unit for ginger. By a 'thumb', I mean an average woman's thumb, as my own is my reference point, so bear that in mind if you are a man and/or happen to have large hands. Finely chopped, a thumb should give you 2 tbsp of ginger. Fresh ginger has a smooth, thin skin; wrinkly ginger is ageing ginger.

TAMARIND

You can buy tamarind as a ready-made paste, which, if you're unlucky, will look like diluted tar and taste of nothing in particular. Block tamarind, with or without seeds, from an Asian grocery shop is far tastier and is easy to use (see Tamarind Sauce, p.128). Sometimes you can buy whole pods of tamarind. These are delicious eaten as a fruit, but unless they are very tart, they will be less suitable for these recipes.

AVOCADOS

Few things are more off-putting than hard, flavourless avocados. Use nice ripe ones: the fruit should give slightly when you press the top near the stem. I like the nutty-flavoured, crocodile-skinned ones myself.

LEMONS, LIMES AND ORANGES

When using citrus zest, I prefer organic fruits because the skins are usually unwaxed and untreated. For just juice, regular fruits are fine.

TOMATOES

Use flavourful, ripe tomatoes to get the best out of a recipe. A few of the cooked dishes ask for canned tomatoes. Substituting fresh for canned will alter both flavour and texture. Tomato paste (purée) is very concentrated and comes in tiny cans.

ONIONS

Red onions are specifically asked for when needed. If a recipe simply says 'onion', you can assume that it is an ordinary brown-skinned one with white flesh, also referred to as 'white' onions in this book. Spring onions or scallions are used in their entirety, unless only the green or white part is requested.

POTATOES

An all-purpose, fairly floury potato is best in most cases, unless otherwise stated. Waxy potatoes are less suitable. If you are reusing leftover boiled potatoes instead of cooking them specially, use scant 10 per cent less than the given raw weight.

TAHINI OR TAHINA

An oily paste made from sesame seeds, it adds loads of flavour to North African and Middle Eastern dishes. I use the light-coloured kind. There is generally always a layer of oil at the top of the jar. Just stir this back into the paste every time before you use it. If you live in a warm climate and don't use the tahini often enough, it might be a good idea to refrigerate it after opening, to prevent it from turning rancid.

SOY SAUCE

Unless otherwise stated, I usually use Japanese-style soy sauce. It has a pure and pronounced flavour and a little goes a long way, especially if you buy a good brand. *Kecap manis* is sweet, thick Indonesian soy sauce.

FISH SAUCE

Use your own favourite brand. Leng, a Cambodian grocer, has assured me most fervently that the price is not necessarily an indication of quality, nor is it a guarantee.

SALTFISH

Salted cod, once a staple of the poor around the world, has become very expensive – if you can get real cod at all. Unless you happen to live in Portugal, the saltfish (*bacalao*) you buy is likely to be a cheaper and sometimes more sustainable kind of fish. It comes as whole fillets or small blocks sawn off from a huge slab of compressed fish. Saltfish always needs to be desalted and it loses a lot of weight along with the salt, so be prepared to end up with about 66 per cent of your packaged weight. Here's how I do it: take a 450g pack of saltfish. Shake off any obvious salt and put the fish in a large pan. Rinse the fish well in cold water, draining and refilling several times, until no more salt comes away in the water. Add 2 litres cold water. Bring to the boil, reduce the heat and simmer uncovered for 15 minutes. Drain. Taste a piece from the thickest part. If it still tastes very salty, repeat the process. Drain and use, or keep well sealed in the fridge for up to a few days, until needed. Bits left over from a recipe make a great addition to scrambled eggs and egg and spring onion fried rice.

EQUIPMENT

WEIGHING AND MEASURING

As always, I urge you very strongly to use scales for accuracy. Small amounts are given in tsp and tbsp. A tsp is 5ml and a tbsp 15ml. Spoons are always level, unless otherwise stated.

TAWA OR GRIDDLE

Indians use a *tawa* for *roti*, but they differ around the world. Subcontinental Indians prefer a slightly concave model, whereas Caribbean families use a perfectly flat one. A well-seasoned or non-stick griddle is also ideal for the flatbreads and wraps that are cooked in a dry pan.

FRYING PAN

When a size is given for a frying pan, e.g. 23cm, this refers to the base, where the food will be cooked. Maddeningly, manufacturers seem to focus on the top measurement on their labels and stamps, which is no help, as the base is always a few centimetres less. A non-stick pan makes life very easy for pancakes. Failing that, use a well-seasoned cast-iron one.

PANS FOR DEEP-FRYING

A deep and sturdy pan is a necessity. It needn't be anything special, as long as it is suitable for deep-frying. I alternately use a large stainless-steel wok and a cheap enamelled black pan. These pans heat differently. The black one attracts and holds heat and can overheat if you're not careful. The stainless-steel one is slower but steadier. This is why you need a thermometer. If you prefer to use an automatic deep-fat fryer, please do.

THERMOMETER

Unless you are a very practised deep-fryer, it is best to use a thermometer rather than just guess the temperature of your oil. It goes without saying – but I'm still saying it – that different foods require different temperatures. Oil that is too cool will make your food greasy, and too hot oil will brown the outside very attractively, while the inside may be quite raw.

DRAINING SPOON

A mesh draining spoon or small shallow basket, the kind that is called a 'spider', is ideal for removing fried articles from oil as it drains almost spontaneously. A slotted spoon will retain more oil.

BRUSH

I use a silicone brush for greasing frying pans. It can withstand far higher temperatures than natural bristle ones which tend to singe. Avoid synthetic bristles as they will simply melt.

TURNING SPATULA

A thin, flat spatula with a large surface area is my own choice for both flatbreads and pancakes, but some people prefer the special wooden ones that look like palette knives. Use whatever works best for you and bear in mind that thick spatulas with upraised ends may damage the more delicate pancakes.

MIXING SPATULA

Flexible silicone spatulas will enable you to scrape the batter very effectively from the sides of the bowl, so that you don't lose any.

WHISK

Any sturdy wire whisk will do for general purposes. I like balloon whisks because they mix more lightly and, as the wires are further apart, not much sticks in the middle of the whisk as often happens with slimmer models.

SILICONE MAT

This remains my favourite and best-used piece of kitchen equipment. It is good for so many things, especially for rolling out dough very thinly without tearing or sticking. I cannot recommend it highly enough. Because of the non-stick properties, you will need little to no flour for dusting and your flatbreads and doughs will be all the better for it.

ROLLING PIN

Your favourite rolling pin will be fine. I use wooden ones that have seasoned themselves to non-stick over the years. I do find that smaller items are best rolled with a smaller, slimmer pin, as you can then manoeuvre better and with more finesse than with a larger kind.

INDEX

BIBLIOGRAPHY

Al-Hashimi, Miriam. *Traditional Arabic Cooking*. Reading: Garnet Publishing Ltd, 1993

Benanni-Smires, Latifa. *La Cuisine Marocaine*. Casablanca: La Societé d'Édition et de Diffusion Al Madariss, 2004

Besa, Amy and Romy Dorotan. *Memories of Philippine Kitchens*. New York: Stewart, Tabori & Chang, 2006

Chinese Dim Sum. Taipei: Chin Chin Publishing Co. Ltd, 1993

Ching Lee Sook. *Cook Malaysian*. Singapore: Times Editions, 2003

Cunqueiro, Álvaro and Arceli Filgueira Iglesias. *Galicia: Cocina Tradicional*. La Coruña: Editorial Evergráficas, n.d.

Gergely, Anikó. *The Traditional Hungarian Kitchen*. Budapest: Vince Kiadó, 2000

Halıcı, Nevin. *Nevin Halıcı's Turkish Cookbook*. London: Dorling Kindersley Ltd, 1989

Lambert Ortiz, Elizabeth. *The Complete Book of Mexican Cooking*. New York: Galahad Books, 1967

Maiberg, Ron. *Taste of Israel*. Bnei Brak: Steimatzky Ltd, 1990

Olizon-Chikiamco, Norma. *Filipino Sweets and Snacks*. Hong Kong: Periplus Editions (HK) Ltd, n.d.

Öney Tan, Aylin (ed.). *Gaziantep Cookery: A Taste of Sun and Fire*. Gaziantep: Gaziantep Chamber of Commerce, 2012

Owen, Sri. *Indonesian Food and Cookery*. Totnes: Prospect Books, 1986

Pagrach-Chandra, Gaitri. *Warm Bread and Honey Cake*. London: Pavilion, 2009

Pagrach-Chandra, Gaitri. *Het Nederlands Bakboek*. Utrecht: Kosmos Uitgevers, 2012

ACKNOWLEDGEMENTS

I owe thanks to many people, for many things: for little asides and specific advice; for cooking with me and sharing knowledge so generously; for providing encouragement and feedback and for magnificent hospitality during my travels. Thank you Sri and Roger Owen, Gina Lim, Pia Lim-Castillo, Nevin Halıcı and Caroline Smith. My sister Goutami Indar-Ramnauth, a dedicated sampler of snacks, brainstormed regularly with me, expertly lobbying for the inclusion of many Caribbean titbits. My husband Henk and our children Judy and Leon lived up to their reputations as my best tasters and critics. And my agent Charlotte Bruton once again dealt expertly with everything that needed to be dealt with.

As always, it has been a delight to work with the Pavilion team: commissioning editor Emily Preece-Morrison, who again enthusiastically supported me from beginning to end, copy editor Kathy Steer, designers Georgina Hewitt and Anna Perotti, production manager Laura Brodie and proof-reader Alyson Silverwood. Photographer Keiko Oikawa, food stylist Aya Nishimura and her assistant Xenia von Oswald, together with props stylist Jo Harris, produced the mouth-watering photos.

And although it is self-evident, I'd still like to thank you, dear readers, because without you, there would be no books. Thank you all!